The Rāmāyaṇa in Bengali Folk Paintings

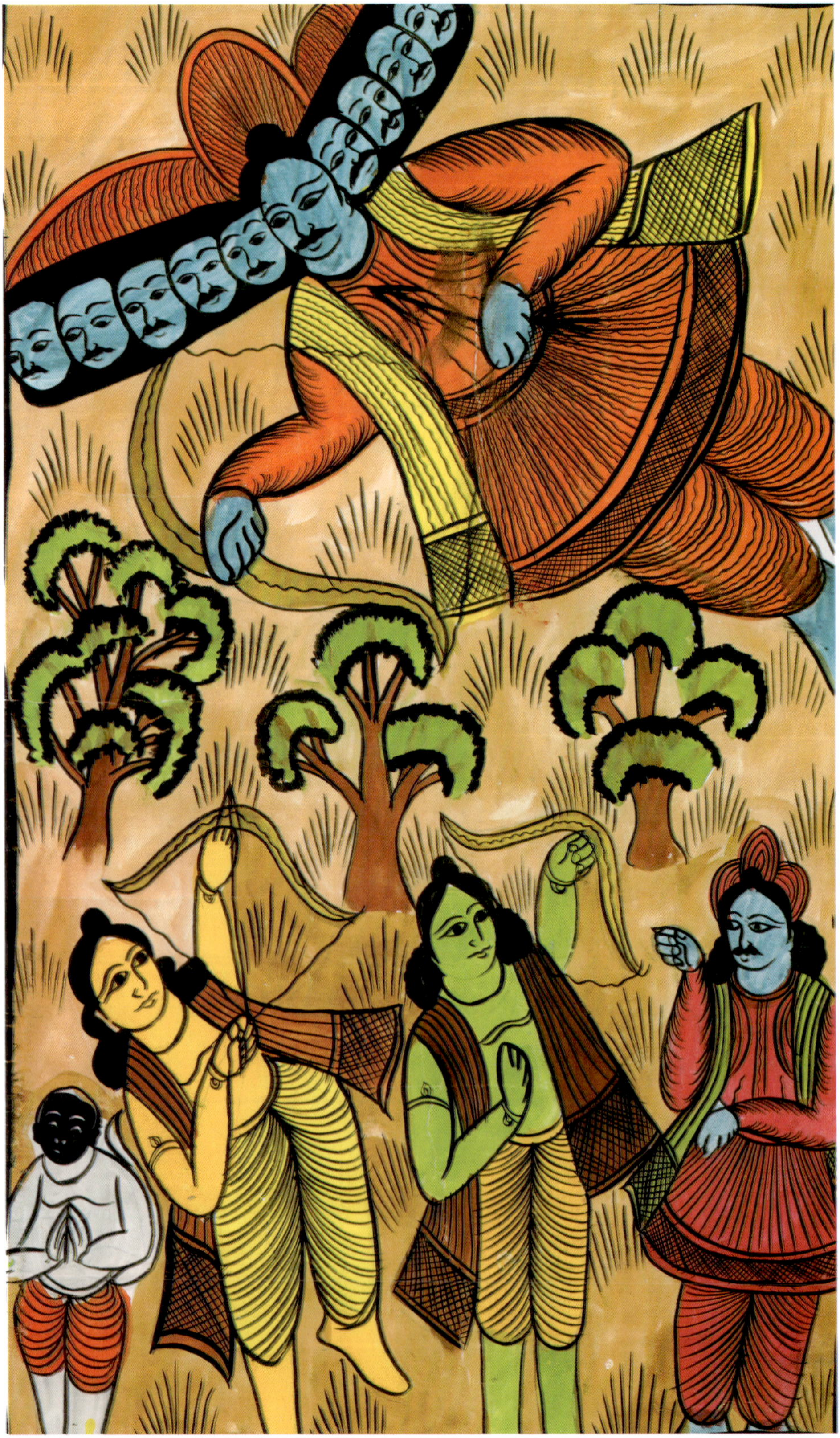

The Rāmāyaṇa in Bengali Folk Paintings

Mandakranta Bose

NIYOGI
BOOKS

Published by

NIYOGI BOOKS

D-78, Okhla Industrial Area, Phase-I
New Delhi-110 020, INDIA
Tel: 91-11-26816301, 49327000
Fax: 91-11-26810483, 26813830
email: niyogibooks@gmail.com
website: www.niyogibooksindia.com

Photograph: Mandakranta Bose

Editor: Upama Biswas
Design: Nabanita Das

ISBN: 978-93-85285-55-4
Publication: 2017

Printed at: Niyogi Offset Pvt. Ltd., New Delhi, India

To my Sonamoni Lily, with love.

contents

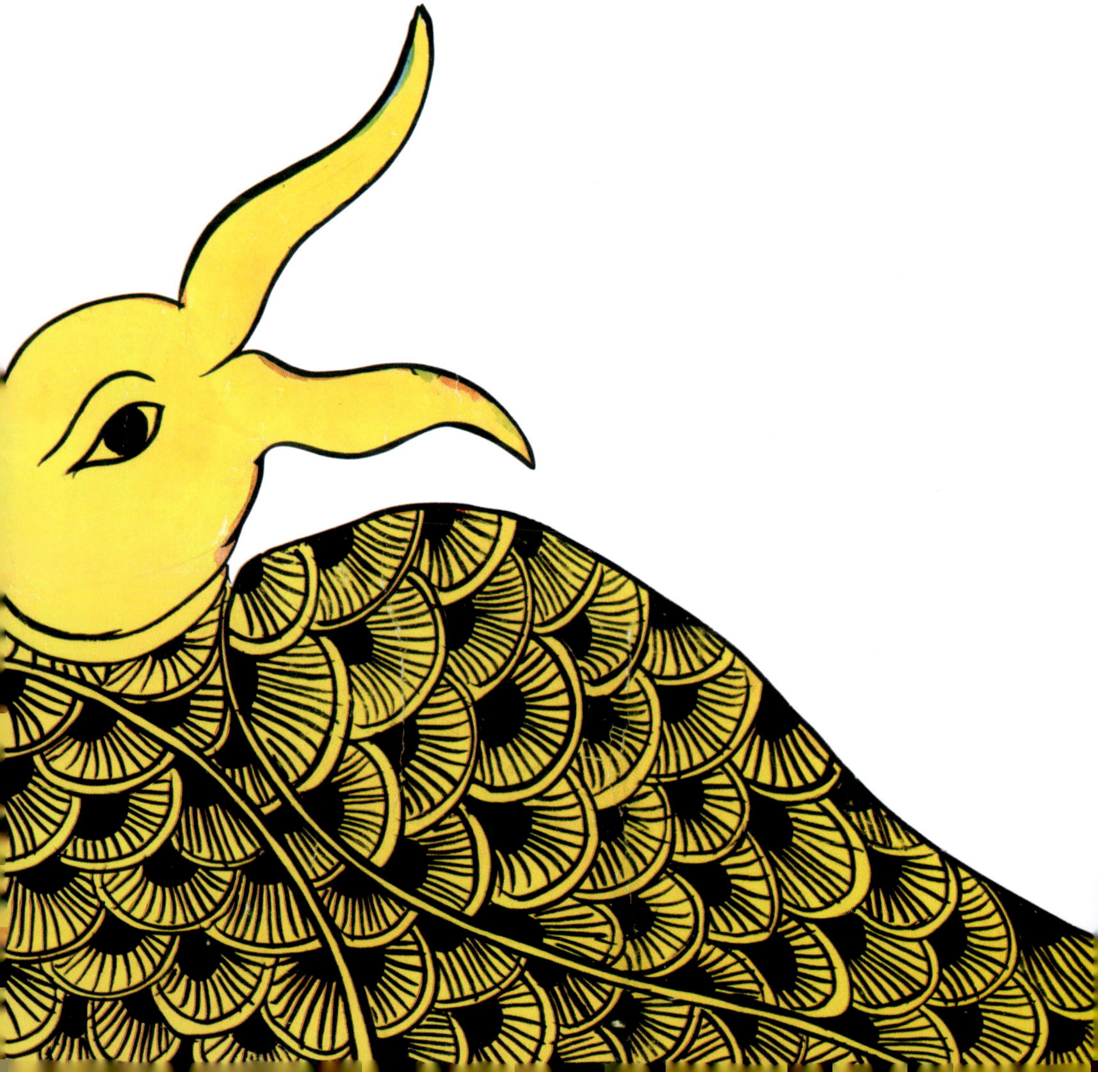

foreword

The *Rāmayāṇa*, without the evil maid Mantharā who provoked Kaikeyī to demand that her son Bharata and not Rāma become the next king of Ayodhya, would come to an abrupt end in the second chapter. Yet, we learn from Mandakranta Bose that this defining *kāṇḍa* has consistently been omitted from the Bengali folk artists' version of the *Rāmāyaṇa*. This seems shocking although there is nothing startling in learning of yet another version of the *Rāmāyaṇa*. Vālmīki's *Rāmāyaṇa* has been translated from Sanskrit into Indian languages and English, in its entirety and abbreviated form, and transcreated in a range of forms including stage dramas, TV serials, movies, short stories, novels, comics, and even a coloring book. Excluding versions of the *Rāmāyaṇa* found in Cambodia, Thailand, Myanmar, Indonesia, and other countries of Southeast Asia—just a list of the languages A. K. Ramanujan wrote "makes one gasp" [1] – there are still hundreds of

1 A. K. Ramanujan, "Three Hundred Rarniiyanas: Five Examples and Three Thoughts on Translation," in *The Collected Essays of A.K. Ramanujan*, ed. Vinay Dharwadker (Delhi: Oxford University Press, 1999), p. 133.

versions. And, while many of these versions have been documented and studied, the *Rāmāyaṇa* of the *paṭuās* of Bengal has not.

A noted Sanskrit scholar, Mandakranta Bose is Professor Emerita at the Institute of Asian Research at the University of British Columbia and Director of the Institute's Centre for India and South Asia Research. Well known for her writings on classical dance and the *Rāmāyaṇa*, I am especially appreciative of Professor Bose's work in women's history: *Faces of the Feminine in Ancient, Medieval and Modern India* (Edited, 2000) and *Women in the Hindu Tradition: Rules, Roles and Exceptions* (2010), which are solidly based on texts and concerned with helping us understand women's lived lives. Her most recent book, a translation of Candrāvatī's *Rāmāyaṇa*, a sixteenth-century text titled *A Woman's Rāmāyaṇa: Candrāvatī's Bengali Epic* (2013), written with her daughter Sarika Priyadarshini Bose, contextualises a remarkable and gendered retelling of the epic.

Always interested in the *Rāmāyaṇa*, Bose first noticed scrolls by the Bengali *paṭuās* in the 1950s, returning to them in the 1980s to begin systematic and determined research on how they presented this story. This was when I first became interested in scroll paintings, attracted by their portrayal of social issues. Later, I was smitten by portrayals of Śūrpaṇakhā telling Rāvaṇa of her humiliation, Jaṭāyu's struggle to save Sītā, and Aṅgada's meeting with Rāvaṇa. Bose's *The Rāmāyaṇa in Bengali Folk Paintings* provides the context in which to understand the *paṭuās' Rāmāyaṇa*, a distinct Bengali folk retelling of this ancient story.

The history of the *paṭuās* or "chitrakars" (indigenous painters) of Bengal is difficult to write without acknowledging gaps in documentation. Most historians recognize ancient forms of storytelling with the aid of picture scrolls but have difficulty connecting twentieth-century *paṭacitra* artists to their ancient ancestors. David McCutchion and Suhrid Bhowmik cite the thirteenth-century *Brahmavaivarta Purāṇa* as the first textual reference to these artists. McCutchion and Bhowmik refer to angry Brahmins declaring that the *paṭuās'* "pictures and images were erroneous" and discrediting the community.[2] Contemporary folk artists offer imaginative retellings of their origins. Frank Korom has related Gurupada's story of how, two to three thousand years ago, some very clever villagers used a glass [mirror] to destroy a rapacious demon. They decided the best way to broadcast their victory would be to paint it and then travel from village to village telling and showing others what had happened. According to Gurupada, people paid them with food and coins but soon became bored with the demon story and asked for new tales. This was the beginning of *paṭuās* and *paṭas*.[3]

Bose begins this erudite but accessible book by relating her interest in these paintings and decision to collect *Rāmāyaṇa paṭas*. Documenting the interest of famous collectors such as Gurusaday Dutta and David McCutcheon, Bose provides both the history of the study of *paṭas* and what we know about the history of the artist community. In the second chapter, Bose discusses the painting tradition, the depiction of the *Rāmāyaṇa* in art, regional *Rāmāyaṇas*, the role of the *Rāmāyaṇa* in Bengal, the history of the *paṭuās*, and the status of these artists today. Her point is that these folk artists, while mostly illiterate and closely linked to other rural subalterns, have been influenced by the literary and artistic culture of Bengal. Their telling of the *Rāmāyaṇa* is based on Kṛttivāsa's *Rāmāyaṇa* and influenced by the *Rāmāyaṇa*s of Rāmprasāda and Jagadrāma, a father and son team, and Dāśarathī Rāya, but has its own distinct features. The third chapter includes translations of two songs, composed by Niranjan Chitrakar from Habichak and Dukhushyam Chitrakar from Naya, that accompany the scrolls and

2 David J. McCutchion and Suhrid K. Bhowmik, *Patuas and Patua Art in Bengal* (Calcutta: Firma KLM Private Ltd., 1999), p. 10-11.

3 Frank J. Korom, *Village of Painters: Narrative Scrolls from West Bengal* (Santa Fe: University of New Mexico, 2006) p. 36-39.

two folk songs about the *Rāmāyaṇa*. Although the *paṭuās'* art is more widely disseminated than their songs, the songs illustrate, as Bose so aptly puts it, their "empathy with the disempowered of the world."

These three chapters form the background necessary to appreciate the *paṭuās' Rāmāyaṇa* presented in chapter 4. This is my favourite chapter as Bose presents the *Rāmāyaṇa* as the *paṭuās* sing and paint it, using frames from different artists to tell the story. She persuasively argues that the *Rāmāyaṇa* of the *paṭuās* is as vivid and nuanced as any other telling and deserves attention for its interesting and unique features. Certain events are left out and others are given prominence. Similar to Candrāvatī's *Rāmāyaṇa*, which she knows so well, Bose finds considerable attention to and sympathy for Sītā. She urges us to think about this departure from the written text and ponder whether it suggests something about the folk culture from which these scrolls emanated and found an audience. Although not specifically addressing gender, Mandakranta Bose raises fascinating questions about a folk culture that may have had a kinder, more sympathetic view of women's plight than found in Vālmīki's and Kṛttivāsa's *Rāmāyaṇas*.

Geraldine Forbes
Distinguished Teaching Professor Emerita
State University of New York, Oswego

preface

My introduction to a unique type of folk painting of Bengal was through a colourful painted scroll depicting Sītā's abduction by Rāvaṇa and the mythical bird Jaṭāyu's struggle to death with him to rescue her. Painted with vegetable and other indigenous dyes in a vibrant and colourful style on handmade paper, it was a paṭacitra, a narrative painted sequentially on several frames. I was acquainted with the term paṭa but had never seen one before. Although the painting depicted a well-known episode from the *Rāmāyaṇa*, the abduction of Sītā (Sītāharṇa), it looked very different from other folk paintings I knew, such as the Kalighat paintings of gods, goddesses, women, birds and animals. It was not done in the style of Jamini Roy either, which at that time, in the 1950s and 1960s, was very popular. I saw this unique piece at a friend's home in Calcutta (now Kolkata) in the late 50s.[1] This friend came from an old Kolkata family that had lived in Kolkata for over almost 300 years, since the city's birth, and was well acquainted

1 I have used the current spelling, Kolkata, throughout except for citations, for which I have followed the spelling as given on the title page.

with the history and culture of the towns and villages of Bengal. It was the family's long-established interest in Bengali folk paintings that led an ancestor of my friend to acquire the painting. The family had collections of many such artefacts not usually seen in other Bengali homes. I had not seen any other folk painting in that style anywhere else and could not learn more about the style at that time.

Shortly after this encounter I went to England to study and returned to Kolkata a few years later, eventually moving with my family to Canada, which has now become my home in the West. However, Kolkata too has remained my home and I visit the city every year. But even through many visits to Kolkata I did not come across any other paṭacitra until the late 1980s when, to my surprise, I found that almost every academic friend of mine who was interested in India, especially in Bengal, possessed at least one such painting. Later, I gathered that, to our good fortune, this folk art had begun to draw serious interest from art collectors and academics alike just before it was about to sink into oblivion. The more I looked at these paṭas, the more I was drawn to them as much for their artistic form as for their narrative power. Particularly interested in the representation of the *Rāmāyaṇa* in the arts of India, I began to collect paṭas, focusing on paṭas depicting *Rāmāyaṇa* episodes and characters. The pages that follow comprise the result of my attempt to understand how this vibrant art form communicates the complexities of an ancient epic.

acknowledgements

This has been a long-deferred labour of love that could not have been completed without the encouragement of many friends and colleagues. Geraldine Forbes has shared with me her rich, life-long experience of the culture of the Bengali-speaking people and especially her knowledge of the paintings this book presents, stretching the ties of a long friendship by letting me use paṭas from her own collection. Frank J. Korom has been similarly open-handed with his deep knowledge of the paṭas and their painters, and has permitted me to use material from his extensive collection. To these sources of aid I have to add the constant support I have received from the team at Niyogi Books, especially Mohua Mitra and Upama Biswas. For technical support with the digitised reproduction of the paṭas, I am grateful to the experts at my university and at the Dominion Blue Reprographics printshop in Vancouver.

I may mention here my fond memory of the late Professor William Smith at a *Rāmāyāṇa* symposium about fifteen years ago in Vancouver. His research on the eastern Indian traditions of the *Rāmāyaṇa*, including the folk paintings of Bengal, remains invaluable. He shared with me his findings, which included articles on paintings that he collected on his visits to eastern region India, particularly Bengal, Orissa and Assam. We discussed plans for working together on Bengali *Rāmāyaṇas*. It is unfortunate that this never came to fruition as he passed away suddenly. His *Rāmāyāṇa Traditions of Eastern India* has given me much inspiration and provided directions to look into this area. He collected different stories, written and oral, and shared a number of them with me. I gratefully acknowledge my indebtedness to him.

This book has had to be completed through a long period of weakened eyesight. It would not have been possible without the constant editorial help of my husband Tirthankar Bose.

introduction

The art of scroll painting goes a long way back in India's cultural tradition. Found in many regional traditions, it has had a particularly rich history in eastern India, especially in parts of Bengal. However, the colonial era proved to be lean times for indigenous cultural forms, especially with the growing influence of art and literature derived from Western models and sensibilities. Yet the same sensibilities eventually came to evoke interest in India's native traditions, leading to attempts at reviving them, including folk cultural traditions. By the early 20th century, both scholars and the general public had begun to take delight in rediscovering indigenous art forms, for example, the folk ballads of eastern Bengal indefatigably collected by Dinesh Chandra Sen, thereby saving them for posterity. The art of paṭa painting was the beneficiary of a similar redemption. The person who brought that about was Gurusaday Dutt, a civil servant, who collected a number of paṭas and other artefacts between 1929 and 1941 and founded a museum in Thakurpukur, a suburb of Kolkata, which has a rare and valuable collection of folk art. Though not widely seen by urban populations, paṭas did draw the attention of collectors and eventually found their way into museums. The Ashutosh Museum at Kolkata University is one such repository. Yet in the first part of the 20th century, the art of paṭa painting was by no means thriving. Despite the efforts of early pioneering lovers of folk culture, there was not much enthusiasm among the general public for the kind of art housed in these collections until much later. Many scholars who lamented the situation noted that the folk arts of India, among them the paṭas of Bengal, were becoming moribund (Bandyopadhyaya, 1972; McCutchion and Bhowmik, 1999). Later in the century, though, the tide began to turn. In the late 1950s and 1960s, British scholar David McCutchion drew attention to this folk art form and many academics became aware of its value. He taught Comparative Literature at Jadavpur University but he must be remembered more for his passion for temple terracotta sculptures and for these folk paintings, many of which he collected while carrying out research on the temple art of Bengal. Although there were a few scholars and art lovers from Bengal who had been collecting these paintings and were highly knowledgeable in Bengal's folk art tradition, it would not be unfair to say that David McCutchion was greatly instrumental in bringing them back to the attention of Bengalis and to many foreign scholars at a crucial time when most of us were about to forget this art form and found little value in it. McCutchion's curiosity and love for temple architecture and the folk arts of Bengal attracted many. Unfortunately, his untimely death in 1970, at the youthful age of 41 years, left many of his findings and thoughts unpublished. Later, some of his friends and colleagues published some of his writings but most of these publications are on English Literature and few on temple or folk art. What we do have of these published writings and letters on the subject give us valuable information. His demise brought to a definite end any possibility of

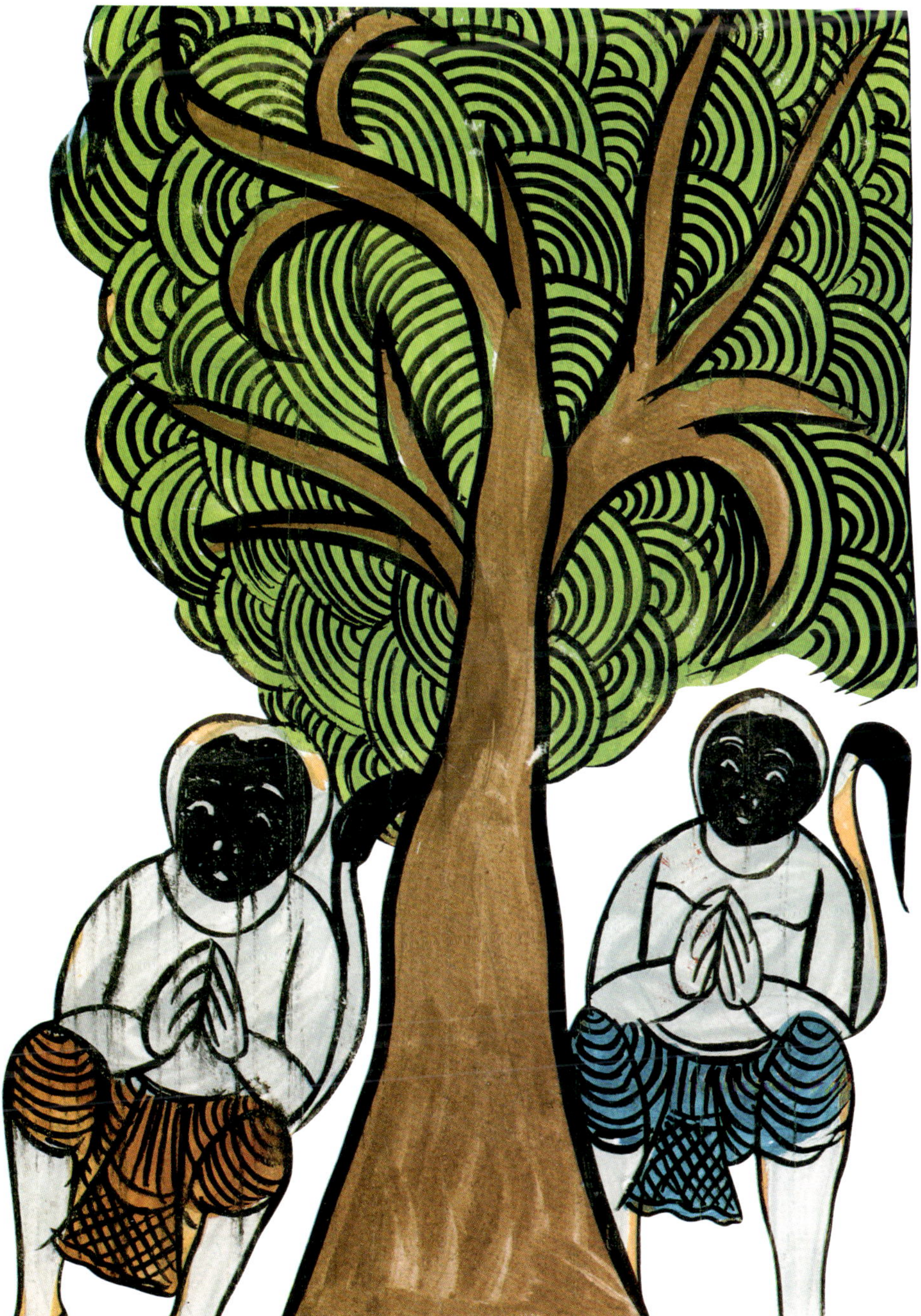

his further contribution to the understanding of this art at that time. He had taken 20,000 pictures of Bengal temples and of folk art, most of which remain unpublished. Part of his collection of paṭas are in a museum in Coventry, England, where he was born, while his material on Bengal temples is in the Victoria and Albert Museum in London. His work in this field still remains unmatched.

Fortunately, from the late 1970s onwards there has been a growing demand for paṭas, and many researchers have been collecting these paintings. This is not exclusively or even mainly an academic venture; art lovers from all walks of life have contributed to the revival of this genre of folk paintings of Bengal. Several cultural groups, such as the Crafts Council of West Bengal and the Daricha Foundation, have taken on the task of preserving and promoting the art of the paṭuās and their livelihood; while an yearly festival of paṭacitras at Naya and Pingla villages in the Medinipur district of West Bengal has become a prized tourist destination. On one of my trips back to Kolkata in the 1990s, I spoke about these painters and their paintings to my niece Tapati Guha Thakurta, noted art historian, who introduced me to several folk painters and their paintings. This was my introduction to the gold mine from which I have drawn material for the present volume.

Having collected a number of painted scrolls, I became curious about their history and began to enquire about the origin and development of the painters as a community, their art form, their lives and their versions of the *Rāmāyaṇa* story. I tried to understand the beauty of their art that has attracted so many from different walks of life. I was aware that folk paintings often resemble both classical and folk art forms, and that examples of such hybridity can be found in every corner of India. Also, a large number of both kinds of paintings focus on stories from the epics and various myths and legends of India, shaped in both form and content by their own regional versions. Yet, it is also true that all folk arts have their distinctive styles, particular to the specific region of the Indian subcontinent from which they come. With the recent rise in enthusiasm and interest in cultural tourism and encouragement from the government, folk arts all over India are doing remarkably well and we are now exposed to a great variety of such art forms. Various folk arts have become more and more accessible to everyone to enjoy and appreciate. As I continued to collect paṭas and to think more searchingly about them, I began to wonder what it was that drew so many people—the painters themselves, their patrons, and academics—to cherish paṭas. How is it that these paintings continue to thrive? Is it their aesthetic power or do they have some special social, economic or religious appeal? And how has their distinct character evolved from ancient times to the present? A historical enquiry was clearly my first task.

References to itinerant painters and storytellers are found in the *Arthaśāstra* of Kauṭilya, where we find that these painters were employed to spy upon the public and on the king's officials while they were wandering through the country (Kauṭilya, 1962). Viśākhadatta's *Mudrārākṣasa* has similar references (Viśākhadatta, 1969: Act 1, verse 16–17). A particularly popular form of painting seems to have been yamapaṭas, that is, painted scrolls displaying the punishments meted out by Yama, the ruler of the underworld, to wrongdoers in their afterlife. Bandyopadhyay discusses yamapaṭas and yamapaṭuās of Birbhum in great detail in his book (Bandyopadhyaya, 1972). A detailed discussion of yamapaṭas and other folk scroll painters from different parts of India with a focus on Rajasthan, Bengal and Bihar is offered by M. L. Varadpande (Varadpande, 1992: II, 116–120). Ananda Coomaraswamy, the well-known 20th-century art historian, commented that some regional paintings are more than simple folk art. In his words, "Rajput painting is essentially an aristocratic folk art, appealing to all classes alike, static, lyrical, and inconceivable apart from the life it reflects" (Coomaraswamy 1985 [1926]: 128)[1] They are indeed highly sophisticated in both conception and composition. The painted scrolls and other paintings produced by rural artists of Bengal are perhaps closer to the aesthetic and social experience of village folk in Bengal and have commanded their interest through centuries. Its attraction for the urban community is more recent. Many researchers often collect them out of anthropological and social curiosity, but many art lovers collect them for their fascination with and genuine love for this particular folk style as well. The method, the style and the use of colour by these folk painters from various regions of Bengal attract artists and art historians equally. But it is also worth emphasising that while as art objects they are immensely attractive, they are certainly not "aristocratic" or high art.

The folk painters of West Bengal, known as paṭuās, have been living by the sale of their paintings, known as paṭacitras or paṭas. At least for the past few centuries, they have been painting scrolls and singing the stories, composing the lyrics in their own words. Singing the *Rāmāyaṇa* story is an important part of their artistic life. I was told that till recently they used to perform only in their own villages and in their neighbouring villages. But today they come to city fairs and visit many city homes to sell their paintings to both local and foreign scholars and visitors. For the past 50 years or more, with government encouragement and sponsorship, these artists have been painting and exhibiting their paintings at various fairs and festivals in and outside Bengal, especially in Delhi. This has brought them continuous exposure beyond their own villages. As such, from the later half of the 20th century they have become well known, indeed popular, among urban

1 Early twentieth century art-historians did not take much notice of village paintings and focused on classical paintings to write the history of Indian Art. It is only in the recent past that anthropologists and art historians have taken a closer interest in folk paintings.

and educated Bengalis as well as in the artistic and the academic world of art lovers within and beyond India. They have also drawn international attention and appreciation. In search of the history of these painters and their art, I have looked at both primary and secondary sources. A number of books are available today, from which a clear pattern of their imagination and beliefs has emerged. Paṭuās paint selected episodes from the *Rāmāyāṇa* and create a unique storyline of their own, drawing mainly from Kṛttivāsa's version of the epic.

As I collected the scrolls and gradually came to know more about them, I felt that the story of the *Rāmāyaṇa* that the paṭuās tell in these scrolls was worth sharing with others, in the hope that this would stimulate more interest in their work and add to our existing knowledge about these artists and their art as well as their literary

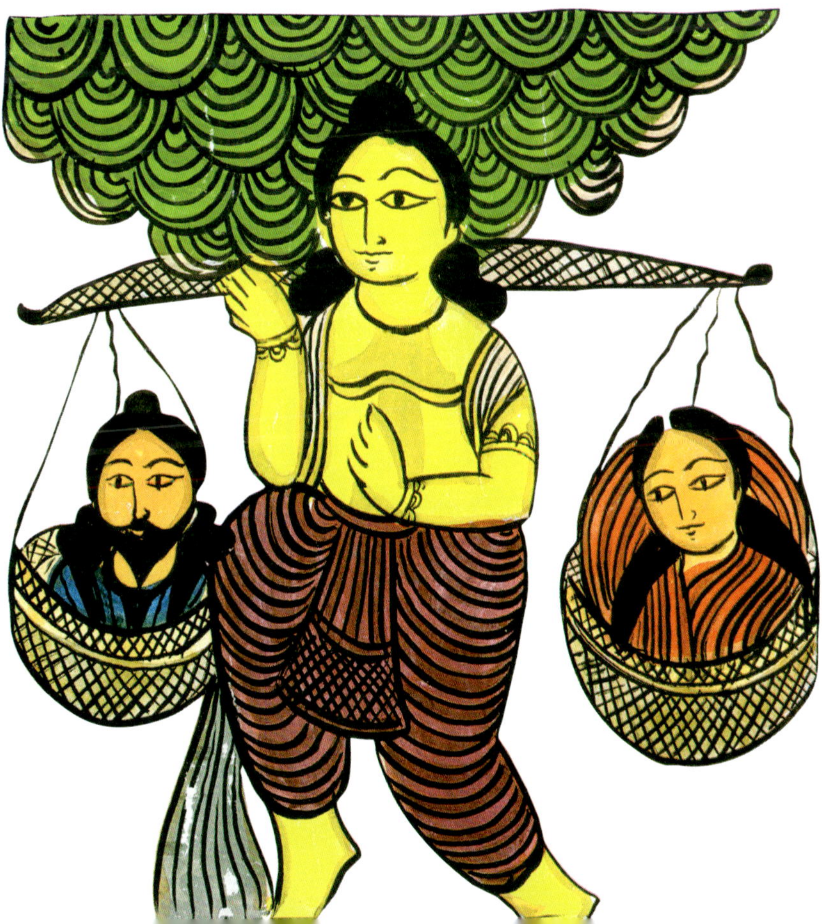

skill, which is considerable, to judge by the songs they compose as accompaniment to the images. Their verbal art is as important as their graphic; indeed, it is common usage with them to describe their work as "paṭa lekha," that is, *writing* a paṭa. I may in passing note that the great modern Bengali painter Abanindranath Tagore described himself as "Aban Thakur, chabi lekhe" (Aban Tagore, writes pictures), in an apparent nod to his roots in the indigenous art tradition of Bengal. On observing the twin art of painting and song that the paṭuās practice, it is evident that the narrative content is of prime importance both to the artists and to their audiences, facilitated by their common knowledge of traditional stories from India's epics, myths and legends, and in modern times, their common experience of public events and concerns. For *Rāmāyaṇa* paṭas the painters draw upon the most commonly known Bengali *Rāmāyaṇa*, the 15th-century version by Kṛttivāsa, leavened with tales from local folk traditions. Their choice of episodes is selective and arranged according to their own plan, but the general sequence is that of Kṛttivāsa, from whom they often use exact lines. But their way of telling the *Rāmāyaṇa* story certainly has a focus different from Kṛttivāsa's. Their choice of episodes is their own and shows what is relevant to them, and this way of telling the story, including these particular emphases, has continued through generations. They skip many major events but the epic they present through their paintings, songs and recitations is a coherent whole. This is the story we are about to observe unfold. My research began with the search for large collections of paṭas. A remarkable collection of Bengal folk paintings is housed in the Gurusaday Musuem in Thakurpukur, which has a rich array of folk paintings and other folk artefacts from all over West Bengal and Bangladesh (Gurusaday Museum, 2008). Ashutosh Museum at the University of Calcutta also has a collection of paṭas and other folk art from the region. Both collections include artefacts from Birbhum, Bankura, Medinipur, Murshidabad, 24 Parganas and other rural parts of the region.[2] These collections exhibit many forms of folk art that tell a number of other myths as well as contemporary, political and social issues. But *Rāmāyaṇa* paṭas remain integral parts of both these collections. The story of the *Rāmāyaṇa* presented here reflects the imagination of a group of paṭuās who continue to paint the same stories for generations. I came to know this group over several years. Their work captured my attention and their pictorial representation of the epic became very dear to me. It is interesting to note that despite choosing the same theme from the epic and producing the same episode again and again, paṭuās from different areas have shown their distinctive tastes and practices in their style, choice of colours and the depiction of expression in the faces of the characters they paint. Speaking about the technique of the paṭuās, Debasish Bandyopadhyay lists the colours they choose and describes how they are made (Bandyopadhyaya, 1972: 5).[3] Jyotindra Jain, the art historian, has discussed their distinct nature at great length in his book on Kalighat paintings (Jain, 1999).

The paṭuās or painters I encountered mostly came from Habichak village in the Medinipur district of West Bengal, but there were others from nearby villages, though all were from Medinipur. I collected many of my paṭas from Niranjan Chitrakar who sang a number of songs on topics such as Sītāharaṇa (abduction of Sītā), Sītā's Agniparīkṣā (Sītā's fire ordeal), Sītā's Pātālapraveśa (Sītā's descent into the earth), and even the Iraq War, painted while the war was still on and presented

2 Paṭuās are also known as citrakars, patidārs and patikars. Folk painters of West Bengal come mostly from Medinipur, Birbhum, Bankura, Purulia, Hoogly and 24 Paraganas; see Ghose, 1981: 75–76.

3 Each region is famous for its distinct style, design and the use of colour. For instance, in Birbhum paṭuās are known to paint and sing to yamapaṭas for centuries, telling the story of the king of death Yama and about his punishment for wrongdoers. Their style is quite distinct as they use white or yellow dots for decoration.

with considerable delight to underscore the difference between Rāma, who brought his dead soldiers back to life, and George W. Bush, who could not. So pervasive is the presence of the *Rāmāyaṇa* in the life of these paṭuās that their perception of even such a purely contemporary event as the Iraq War is coloured by their preoccupation with the *Rāmāyaṇa*. Niranjan's concluding comment is telling: "Rāma was able to bring his army back to life at the end of the war; will Bush be able to revive his soldiers?" Unfortunately, Niranjan died in July 2014, well into his sixties, and we lost a great folk painter and narrator, but I was able to acquire a number of his paintings and record some of his songs. I also collected paṭas from some other paṭuās from the same village and neighbouring ones, from such painters as Golap, Nurjahan, Khokon, Tapan, Kalpana, Banku and others, who painted in a similar stylistic idiom. Besides the stories of Rāma and Sītā, their other favourite subject for painting is the mythical snake goddess Manasā. Other common themes of the paṭuās include a popular village tale about a community of fish, centering on the wedding of a Deriyā fish, cautionary tales about family planning, drug abuse, and social and political topics, each of these paṭas concluding with moral preaching. Other than the doings of Saddam Hussain or George Bush, many contemporary social and political events are followed by the paṭuās as they unfold. Folk painters from other parts besides Medinipur have produced paintings on contemporary issues and famous scandals of the 19th century, such as the affair of the Mahanta (chief priest) of Tarakeshwar and Elokeśī, a female devotee at the temple who was murdered by her husband when he came to know of the affair. There are a number of books by art historians on these paintings as well as on the large number of paṭas produced in Kalighat in turn-of-the-19th-century Kolkata, which comprise a major tradition (Jain, 1999: 48–60). The *Rāmāyaṇa* is not thc principal subject of the paintings studied but is included in their collections.

On studying the paṭas and the songs the paṭuās sing as commentaries in their traditional presentation, it becomes evident that image and song are bound together, forming a composite art form, each enriching the other. Interestingly, in these presentations a recurrent theme is the suffering of women in society. The treatment of women by men and women's vulnerability in a male-dominated society very often takes precedence over other issues in paṭas, and this concern very often finds its focus in Sītā's unrelieved suffering. Other female characters in the *Rāmāyaṇa*, such as Tāṭakā and Śurpaṇakhā are also depicted, though not always with sympathy. Mandodarī is treated more kindly, as a woman rather than as a demoness, as several paintings showing her suggest. Oddly enough, Kaikeyī and Manthara, who are major movers of the epic, do not appear in their paintings nor do the sufferings of Ahalyā or Śabarī. If there are any, I have not come across them. Interestingly, paṭuās seldom spend too much attention on details of battles or killings of individuals. I have not come across any painting of Rāma's killing of Vāli or Śambuka,[4] although one frame—just one out of hundreds—in the paṭas reproduced here does show Vāli, but does not show Rāma killing him. Even the slaying of Rāvaṇa appears only in two or three frames in the range of scrolls I have. But the episode of Rāvaṇa listening to the mutilated Śurpaṇakhā is commonly included and often more than one frame is devoted to his abduction of Sītā. A favourite subject, reflecting the Śākta ethos prevalent in Bengal, is Rāma's worship of Durgā to gain her blessings before going into the final battle with Rāvaṇa. They claim that the selection of episodes from the *Rāmāyaṇa* they depict has been passed on from generation to generation and these episodes have remained important and constant in their artistic vocabulary. During my research, specific patterns of depicting various episodes focusing on women interested

4 A paṭa depicting Vālī is reported to be part of the Victoria and Albert Museum collection of paṭas. I have not been able to see it.

me, especially because of my recent work jointly carried out with my daughter on a critical study and translation of the late 16th-century Bengali *Rāmāyaṇa* composed by the woman poet Candrāvatī. It is the story of Sītā, also of women in general, told by a woman strictly from a woman's perspective. There is reason to believe that this text had a considerable impact on the folk narrative tradition of Bengal in retelling the *Rāmāyaṇa*; one of Niranjan's scrolls definitely bears this out. This is only one reason why these scrolls need sustained enquiry.

A number of art historians and anthropologists have written on these paintings, the painters, their lives, their origins, their history and their painting styles, comparing them with Indian classical art and other Indian folk painting traditions.[5] As a student of literature, my approach takes a literary perspective, which clearly shows that material from widely known versions of the *Rāmāyaṇa* has combined with local legends to influence our painters. Obviously, the painters grew up listening to the recitation of this Bengali *Rāmāyaṇa*. Other literary traditions of Bengal also remain vital to this tradition to survive, especially the *Candrāvatī Rāmāyaṇa*. The painted *Rāmāyaṇa* scrolls here depict stories told by a group of village painters who are influenced by the oral as well as the literary traditions of Bengal. While the work of art historians and sociologists have enriched our understanding of the paṭuās, I believe the story of the *Rāmāyaṇa* through the lenses of these folk painters of Bengal, viewed from a literary perspective, adds as much to our understanding of the *Rāmāyaṇa* as to our appreciation of the cultural life of rural West Bengal and Bangladesh.

5 Major figures in this enterprise are: Gurusaday Dutt, David McCutchion, Suhrid Bhowmick, Tarapada Santra, Benoy Ghose, Debashish Bandyopadhyay, Frank Korom, Geraldine Forbes, Kavita Singh, to mention only some of many contributors to the field.

THE NARRATIVE TRADITION OF INDIAN PAINTING AND THE RĀMĀYAṆA

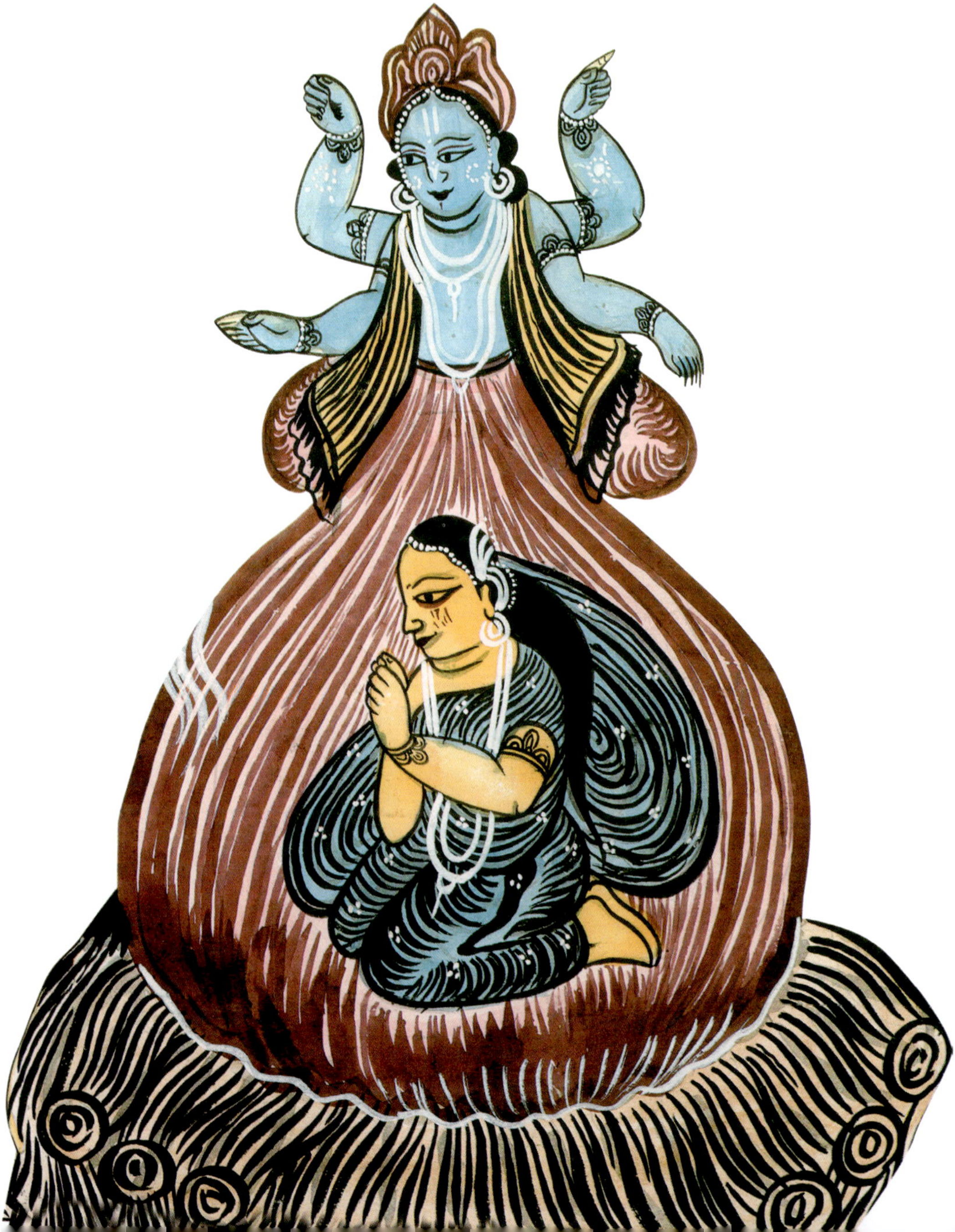

The art of painting, known in classical Indian texts as citrakalā or citraśilpa, is an ancient tradition and telling stories in paintings is an art of long standing in India. It is not known when within its storehouse the folk art of paṭas developed, but there is no doubt that from very early times India had a vibrant tradition of painting along with regimens of artistic training, as evinced by the mention of painting as a valued art in Sanskrit historical, religious and literary texts. Classical Sanskrit works tell us that painting was a favourite pastime of members of ancient royal houses, examples abounding in Sanskrit plays of royal personages practising and enjoying painting. Collections of myths and legends mention painting as an art and as a profession, for example, the *Brahmavaivarta Purāṇa*, as noted later. Painting was taken seriously enough, so much so that it was the subject of manuals such as the citrasūtra section of the *Viṣṇudharmottara Purāṇa* on the art of painting and sculpture, dating back to the early Common Era. To cite a few examples of the place of painting in court culture from classical Sanskrit plays, we may mention Kālidāsa's *Abhijñānaśakuntalam*, which shows King Duṣyanta gazing at a painting of Śakuntalā and her friends in the hermitage (Act VI, prose after verse 13), and Bhāsa's *Svapnavāsavadattam* (Act VI prose after verse 11), which has a scene in which the portrait of King Udayana and Queen Vāsavadattā at their wedding is presented to King Udayana by Vāsavadattā's maid.

He is overwhelmed with grief as he looks at the life-like painting and remembers his beloved wife Vāsavadattā, believed to have been consumed by a palace fire. In Viśākhadatta's *Mudrārākṣasa,* a messenger enters with a yamapaṭa, a scroll showing the world of Yama (Act I, between verses 16–17).[1] In Bāṇabhaṭṭa's *Harṣacarita*, Canto 5, when Prince Harṣavardhana returns to Thanesvar where his father King Prabhākaravardhana lies dying, he sees on all sides ill omens of death, among which is the display of a painted canvas depicting Yama in his domain (Bāṇabhaṭṭa, 1985: 297).[2] That painting in India is an art of long and prestigious lineage is evident, given that all four plays are believed to have been written sometime between the 4th and 8th centuries. Especially pertinent to the present book are references to yamapaṭas in both *Mudrārākṣasa* and *Harṣacarita*, testifying as they do to its early provenance.[3]

The Rāmāyaṇa in Indian Painting

Pre-modern Indian painting looked to India's vast store of legends and complex religious myths for its subjects. Of these, the *Rāmāyaṇa* has been an endless source of artistic inspiration, exerting an influence as wide as it is deep across India and beyond. It has provided subjects of painting and sculptures in both classical and folk styles to artists all over

1 Paṭuās may still be found in the villages of Birbhum, West Bengal, reciting or singing the narrative of a yamapaṭa, or a scroll showing the domain of Yama, the Lord of Death, often including punishments for wrongdoers; see Bandyopadhyaya 1972: 11.

2 As an interesting and not irrelevant aside I may add that in his book of essays titled *Beast and Man in India*, John Lockwood Kipling states that "one of the most popular pictures sold at fairs is a composition known as *Dharmrāj*, a name of *Yama*, the Hindu Pluto" (Kipling 1904: 111). Kipling's description attests to the continuity of a widespread Indian tradition of exhibiting a painting to the accompaniment of a running exposition.

3 See Krishnamachariar (1974 [1937]: Book 4, "Dṛśyakāvya").

India as well as in most of Southeast Asia, wherever the epic remains popular. The tradition of painting and sculpting the *Rāmāyaṇa* story dates back several centuries, and many temple carvings and murals can be found from the early medieval period. Numerous temples in Myanmar, Cambodia, Indonesia, Laos and Thailand are rich storehouses of murals, paintings and carvings showing the Rāma saga in full or part. As one of many examples of painted scenes from India, we may cite the *Rāmāyaṇa* murals on Mattanchery Palace walls in Kochi, Kerala, which date back to the 16th and 17th centuries. A fine example of bas-relief work is the extensive depiction of scenes from the *Rāmāyaṇa* at the Kantaji Temple in Dinajpur, Bangladesh. A common subject of paintings and carvings on temple walls, the *Rāmāyaṇa* appears occasionally in its entirety in painted or carved form, but more common are individual episodes or just a figure or two. Paintings, of course, also exist on palm leaves and paper, and in illustrated manuscripts.[4] Folk culture is similarly rich in representations of the epic, as extended oral narratives or brief tales, songs and plays. Since the beginning of the 20th century, many such artistic productions, both ancient and modern, have attracted artists, art historians and scholars all over the world. Classical paintings and temple carvings, in particular, have attracted many. The miniature paintings of Rajasthan and the Punjab hills, for instance, are well known and have captivated art lovers for centuries. A notable cache of paintings in this style, representing the *Rāmāyaṇa*, was presented by the British Museum, London, for five months in 2008, from May through September, supplemented by illustrative lectures by major *Rāmāyaṇa* scholars. More recently, in the Spring of 2014, an exhibition of folk paintings of the *Rāmāyaṇa* was held in Leeds, UK, with a popular colouring contest for children for painting the episode

4 An example of illustrated manuscripts is a *Citrarāmāyaṇa* (*Rāmāyaṇa* in painting) from Kerala, executed on palm leaves and dating back to 1522, edited by K. Vijayan (1997, reprinted 2000).

of Sītāharaṇa. Clearly, the *Rāmāyaṇa* continues to be a favourite source of subjects for painting in India, both formal and folk. The attraction of folk art and its systematic appreciation by art historians and art lovers have become an integral part of modern cultural discourse for both academics and lay observers.

The Rāmāyaṇas in Bengali Culture

Given its numerous iterations through time and place, it is wise to note that from medieval times on a great range of variations began to appear in regional versions of the *Rāmāyaṇa* throughout India and Southeast Asia. The 15th-century Bengali *Rāmāyaṇa* by Kṛttivāsa is the best known of many Bengali versions, and it includes several episodes that do not appear in Vālmīki's version but are common subjects of Bengali folk painters. Not only in paintings but also in temple reliefs, *Rāmāyaṇa* stories appear in their own distinctive versions, for example in the terracotta temples of West Bengal, especially in the districts of Hugli, Birbhum, Bankura and the 24 Parganas. Some of these temples still hold celebrations in honour of Rāma and Sītā on special occasions. Temples with terracotta reliefs showing *Rāmāyaṇa* episodes are also found in Bangladesh (Chattopadhyaya, 2008: 72–83; Bose, 2010: 25–26). Of literary versions, there have been many, down to the 19th century. A striking example of such distinctive renditions of the Rāma saga in the Bengali-speaking regions of India is the 18th-century Bengali work, the *Rāmprasādī Jagadrāmī Rāmāyaṇa,* which advances in its "Puṣkarakāṇḍa" the Śākta worldview and turns Sītā into Kālī, who protects Rāma from the thousand-headed Rāvaṇa (Rāya and Rāya, 1996: 462–464). This allegiance to Devī, the mother goddess who embodies the feminine principle of creation, is reflected in many paṭas that depict Rāma's worship of Durgā to seek her aid in defeating Rāvaṇa. Another example of the individuality of these versions is Dāśarathī Rāya's 19th-century *Rāmayaṇa* in pāñcālī form, which is pointedly critical of Rāma's suspicion regarding Sītā's chastity while in captivity under Rāvaṇa (Rāya, 1997: 112–113). These two were very popular *Rāmāyaṇas* in Bengali during the 19th and early 20th centuries,[5] although I have not come across any paṭas that are entirely based on these texts. Modern printed texts carry many paintings by local artists but usually none by folk painters. The artistic tradition of painted scrolls by folk artists flourished in Bengal's fertile climate of storytelling and painting, drawing upon the literary tradition as well as on local legends. Art and literature grew together in Bengal, a relationship that thrives to this day (Singh, 2011: 64), the *Rāmāyaṇa* proving to be an endless source of creativity.

The *Rāmāyaṇa* traditions of eastern India as found in Assam, Bengal and Orissa have evolved in their distinct ways by absorbing local stories as well as ideological and cultural idioms without altering the basic structure of the *Vālmīki Rāmāyaṇa,* the ādikāvya or the first poem. To Vālmīki's story, Kṛttivāsa introduced episodes and ideas that seem to have been prevalent in Bengal and eastern India in general. In general, authors of the *Rāmāyaṇas* of Bengal composed after Krttivāsa's version followed his narrative, as did folk painters in choosing *Rāmāyaṇa* episodes for the scenes they painted. Other sources used by painters are not unknown, one being the *Rāmcaritmānas* of Tulsidās, of which there is an illustrated manuscript from Mahishadal, in Murshidabad district, currently in the Ashutosh Museum of Calcutta University (Santra, 2011: 50–51). It is believed that a royal family of that region originally came from Uttar Pradesh and under their queen's instruction the manuscript was written in the Avadhi language in the Nagari script. The style of the paintings in this manuscript is different from that of most Bengali folk

5 See Bose, 2004: 119-121 for a list of Bengali *Rāmāyaṇas*.

paintings, being closer to the Orissan style of folk painting, which may be accounted for by Mahishadal's proximity to Orissa (Santra, 2011: 219–228). These paintings, however, are exceptions to the common narrative and artistic style of the *Rāmāyaṇa* paintings of Bengal and have left no discernible influence on the latter.

Historically, Bengal has known the *Rāmāyaṇa* in four distinct forms, its hold on Bengal derived from the religious ideology of medieval India. The immense popularity and influence of the *Rāmāyaṇa* throughout India owed much to the bhakti movement that swept through North India from the 15th century onwards. While one school of bhakti centred on Śiva, the other focused on Viṣṇu, and it was this latter strand of theology that inspired devotees to view Rāma as Viṣṇu or Nārāyaṇa, the Supreme Divinity, and Sītā as his consort Lakṣmī. The most powerful literary expression of this equation appears in Tulsīdās's *Rāmcaritmānas*, but this was preceded in Bengal by Kṛttivāsa's *Rāmāyaṇa* and followed by many versions embodying different bhakti readings of the epic, sometimes altering the object of worship. Both Vaiṣṇava and Śakta devotional views influenced the culture of Bengal, expressed in traditions of reciting and listening to the Rāma saga and depicting parts of it in paintings, sculptures and temple carvings. These depictions, verbal, musical and graphic, took four forms:

a) Textual versions of the entire or partial story
b) Recitations and songs
c) Bas-reliefs on temple walls
d) Paintings

Of these, we are concerned here mainly with the painted scrolls or paṭas, but a brief survey of the representations of the *Rāmāyaṇa* would set the background to the paṭas, especially the narrative versions, for it is upon these that the painters have traditionally drawn.

❄ a) Textual versions

The formal literary tradition of the Bengali language has left a major impact on Bengali rural culture, including many Bengali versions of the *Rāmāyaṇa*, some of which were derived from Sanskrit *Rāmāyaṇas*. Some are partial versions of the epic, based on particular episodes. Before the arrival of printing, the texts existed in manuscript form and were both read and recited by kathakas or storytellers and by Brahmin pandits at religious and social gatherings. The best known and most influential of the Bengali *Rāmāyaṇas* is the 15th-century work by Kṛttivāsa, mainly based on Vālmīki's Sanskrit version, and similarly in

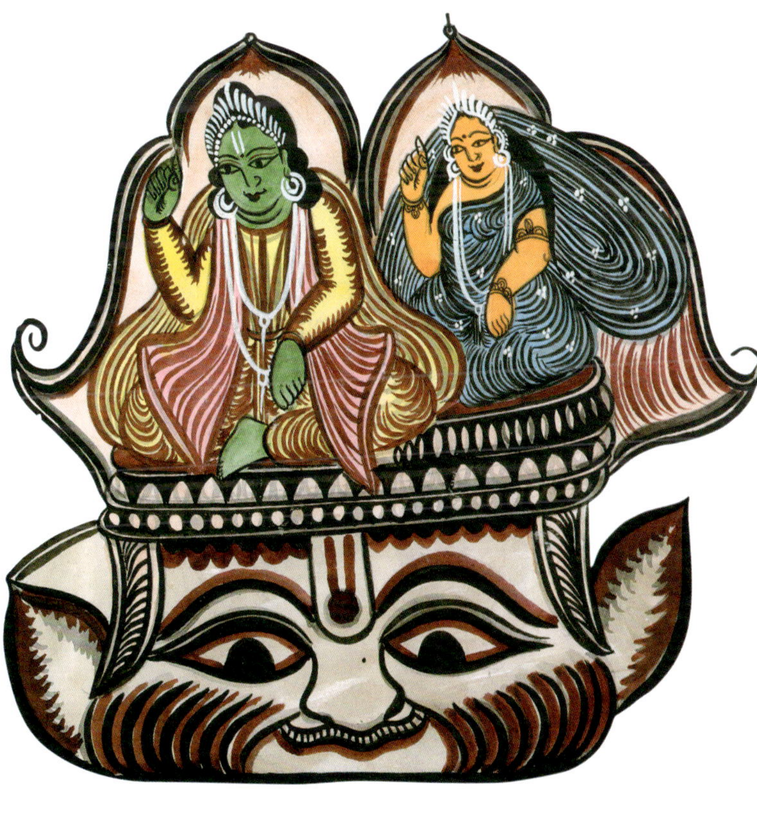

seven parts. Many more versions followed his poem between the 15th and 19th centuries, more than thirty in number (Sen, 1920; Bose, 2004: 119–121), though not all of them tell the entire story, opting rather for selected episodes. Among several shorter versions of the epic one that stands out is by the 16th-century woman poet Candrāvatī, who turns her story into a dirge for Sītā and partly for Mandodarī (Bose & Bose, 2010: "Introduction").

Through centuries these texts have been read and heard by vast numbers of people and have deeply influenced their social beliefs and imaginative productions. While the epic's narrative framework has mainly followed Vālmīki's Sanskrit text, regarded as India's ādikāvya, much new matter has been added by later authors from local and folk narratives, sometimes altering the epic's ethical, theological or emotional bearings. For instance, Candrāvatī's version redirects the reader from male heroism in redeeming the world to women's sad fate in a man's world, while the *Rāmāyaṇa* of Rāmprasāda and Jagadrāma alters the story from a Vaiṣṇava to a Śākta text. Other than reading versions, there have appeared literary dramas, folk plays, yātrās and musical dance dramas based on the *Rāmāyaṇa* theme. Two of the best-known renditions are dance dramas cum musical plays by Rabindranath Tagore; one is *Vālmīkipratibhā*, which celebrates Vālmīki's awakening to poetic inspiration, and the other is *Kālamṛgayā*, a poetic account of the hunting trip during which Daśaratha killed Sindhu, the son of a blind sage and his blind wife, whose curse upon the childless king proved to be a fortunate retribution because it initiated a chain of events that led to the birth of his son Rāma.

❄ b) Recitations and songs

Readings and expositions of sacred texts by Brahmin priests and scholars, and recitations, often musical, of popular tales by bards and storytellers were a vital part of rural life in Bengal from early times. From medieval times, soon after the appearance of Kṛttivāsa's *Rāmāyaṇa*, readings and recitations from it became widespread and highly popular, usually delivered in a rhythmic and musical style. People who could not read, which meant most women, would often memorise parts of the text from what they had heard and would re-tell the stories, to children in particular. There arose a strong oral tradition of singing or reciting individual episodes or even the entire epic on special religious occasions through several days, a practice that continues to this day though not as commonly as before.

❈ c) Bas-reliefs on temple walls

As elsewhere in India, temples in Bengal have a long and rich history of artistic production, both in their architecture and sculptural decoration, in the form, mainly, of relief carvings. The temples of Bengal are distinguished especially by the wealth of bas-relief in terracotta, depicting sacred and mythological subjects, including scenes from the *Rāmāyaṇa*, such as Rāma shooting arrows at Rāvaṇa or Rāma seated on his throne, attended by Sītā and Lakṣmaṇa. A temple with a particularly rich display of such scenes is the Kantaji Temple in Dinajpur, Bangladesh.

❈ d) Paintings

The predominant form of *Rāmāyaṇa* paintings in Bengal is the paṭa or multi-frame scrolls painted by rural artists as visual counterparts of spoken or sung narratives. Paintings of single figures or groups, such as Rāma and Sītā, or particular scenes executed for private patrons or illustrations of manuscripts have enjoyed little importance in Bengal, in contrast with the Pahari or Mewari traditions of miniatures and manuscripts. The Bengali paṭuās drew upon Bengali versions of the epic, mainly Kṛttivāsa's *Rāmāyaṇa* and also locally circulating stories, which sometimes led to the addition of personal interpretations and judgments to the narrative. For rural viewers and audiences, *Rāmāyaṇa* paṭas have been historically no less important a source of knowledge of the epic than community readings and recitations and thus have contributed to moulding the Bengali ethos.

THE BENGALI PAṬUĀS: HISTORY, BACKGROUND AND STYLE

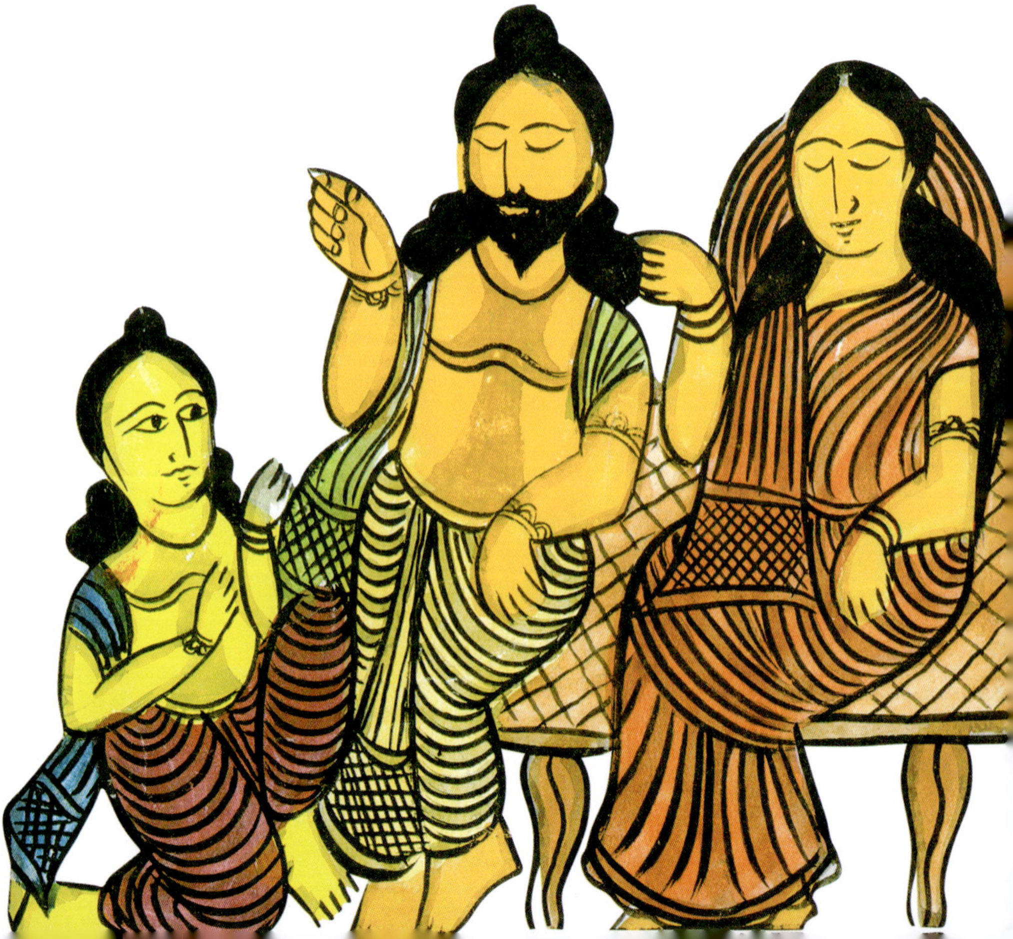

While painters from different regions of Bengal use Kṛttivāsa in common as their narrative source, they do have their distinctive styles both in their emphasis on episodes and in their artistic style. For instance, painters from Medinipur district work on common themes and episodes and use similar colours and designs. Favourite subjects of the Medinipur paṭuās are Sindhuvadha (Daśaratha's hunting trip and his killing of Sindhu by mistake), Tāḍakāvadha (the killing of rākṣasī Tāḍakā), the humiliation of Śūrpaṇakhā, the drawing of Lakṣmaṇarekhā (Lakṣmaṇa marking a protective magic circle around Sītā when Sītā sends him away to help Rāma), Sītāharaṇa (the abduction of Sītā),[1] Jaṭāyuvadha (the killing of Jaṭāyu, the mythical bird), Devīpūjā (Rāma's worship of Devī Durgā to seek her blessings), Mandodarī being tricked by Hanumān to give away the secret of Rāvaṇa's prāṇavāyu (lit: breath of life), Sītā's Agniparīkṣā (Sītā's fire ordeal), and Sītā's Pātālapraveśa (Sītā's descent into the earth). The choice of these episodes suggests how strong Kṛttivāsa's influence is, for some of the episodes, such as the drawing of the Lakṣmaṇarekhā and Rāma's attempt to seek Devī Durgā's blessings, are his inventions. These are among the most common and favourite subjects of folk paintings from Bengal and

1 This is a favourite subject of the painters and appears on many scrolls in my collection and those of others.

are reproduced every year by painters in their scrolls. Interestingly, I find that in my collection the episode of Rāvaṇavadha (the killing of Rāvaṇa) appears as a part of Sītā's rescue effort rather than by itself. It is depicted on several frames in which the focus is less on Rāvaṇa's death than on Sītā's rescue or the lament of Rāvaṇa's widows, especially Mandodarī's plight. I have not come across any painting of Vālivadha or Śambukavadha (the killings of Vāli or Śambuka) by these painters. In my collection of scrolls painted by Golap and his family members, six kāṇḍas of the epic appear but not the uttarakāṇḍa or the seventh section. No scrolls show Kaikeyī or Mantharā, nor do they show the tales of Vālī or Śambuka. In a personal communication, Professor Geraldine Forbes, who has a substantial collection of paṭas from other paṭuās from other districts of Medinipur, has informed me that she does not have any paṭa depicting those episodes either. The collection of Professor Frank Korom, another authority, also contains paṭas on the most popular subjects, such as Sindhuvadha,[2] Sītāharṇa and Agniparīkṣā, but not Kaikeyī, Mantharā, Vālī or Śambuka. One may understand why the episodes of Vālī and Śambuka, which bring no credit to Rāma, would be dropped by the painters, but it is not clear why they would leave out the episode of Kaikeyī and Mantharā, considering its crucial role in telling Rāma's story.

Telling the story is of prime value. To serve the narrative function of the paṭas, each episode is related through a sequence of frames, numbering six to nine, decorative borders surrounding each frame. Different families choose their own signature designs to border the frames, which distinguish their paṭas from the work of other paṭuā families. Paṭuās sign their names and sometimes their village locations on the back of their paintings, which was not done in earlier times but

2 The Sindhuvadha episode also touched Rabindranath Tagore's imagination and he wrote a musical drama on the theme titled *Kālamṛgayā* ("The ill-fated hunting trip"). It is still a popular item on the Bengali stage.

is now common practice. The details of the episodes they depict come from Bengali *Rāmāyaṇas* although the overall plot is from the *Vālmīki Rāmāyaṇa*.[3] But all these episodes have been filtered through their imagination and the embellishments and elaborations are their own.

Who are the Paṭuās: Legends of Origins

The folk painters of India from rural areas, many of them painters of narrative scrolls, were recognised as a class by themselves, quite different from court painters and aristocratic practitioners of painting, and probably more numerous. Evidence of their existence occurs in Kauṭilya's *Arthaśāstra*, which mentions itinerant state spies called sañcāras in Book 1, sec. 7, chap. 11, rule 4; while Book 4, sec. 71, chap. 4, rule 2 includes among them painters who depict on their scrolls the punishments meted out by Yama to wrongdoers.[4] A more elaborate legend of the origin of painters as a caste appears in the *Brahmavaivarta Purāṇa*, a medieval puranic text, which attests to painting being an established profession in medieval times. This text relates how the divine architect Viśvakarmā desired an apsarā named Ghṛtāci but as she would not yield to him on that day, he cursed her to be born into a śudra family, while she in turn cursed him to be born as a mortal. Inexplicably, in her śudra form she came to bear Viśvakarmā nine sons, who became the progenitors of all artisans and craftsmen, but the stigma of being born to a śudra woman consigned them and their descendants to a lower caste. Their nine caste names assigned by occupation were: Mālyakāra, Karmakāra, Śaṅkhakāra, Kuvindaka, Kumbhakāra,

3 The elaborate story of the killing of Sindhu by Daśaratha is not found in Vālmīki, nor that of Lakṣmaṇa drawing a protective circle around the forest abode of Rāma and Sītā known as the Lakṣmaṇarekhā. They are Kṛttivāsa's invention and repeated by later re-tellers of the *Rāmāyaṇa* (Bose, 2015: 235–238).

4 Kauṭilya is believed to have lived in the early Common Era, between 1st and 3rd centuries (Olivelle, 2013: "Introduction").

Kaṁsakāra, Sūtradhāra, Citrakāra and Svarṇakāra (*Brahmavaivarta Purāṇam*, Brahma Khaṇḍa, 1. X. 15–23). Drawing upon this legend, citrakāras or painters trace their lineage back to Viśvakarmā. But the legend has also come to create an identity crisis among the paṭuās in later times by rendering their caste location uncertain, as discussed often and at length in several studies of these artists (Jain, 1999: 48–49; Korom, 2006: 32–45). But there are several other stories that explain their fall into a low-caste position, as often related by the painters themselves. With minor variations, most stories run the same way: in the mythical past, the forebears of the painters failed, while painting, to follow the rules or proper procedures laid down in manuals of painting and general conduct. Instead of using water for their paintbrushes they used saliva to wet them, a practice utterly abhorrent to Hindus. The painters were thus considered to have polluted the paintings, which are expected to be pure and unpolluted. In one account, this offended Śiva who was passing by, and he laid a curse on them, demoting them to a lower social stratum. In other accounts, it was a different god or a sage who was responsible for their fall into a lower caste (Korom, 2006: 33-45). As fallen people they seem to have been rejected by Muslims as well, which has left them in a social limbo. Some of them claim to be Hindus, and some to be Muslims, while some want to belong to neither of these faiths but want to be recognised as an independent "chitrakar jāti" or painter caste. As I have mentioned earlier, from my encounter I gather that today's painters have assumed lifestyles and religious rituals in whatever form that suits them, but they mostly prefer to be identified as members of the chitrakar jāti. But this too is not always the case. Jyotindra Jain mentions that Kalighat paṭuās, who usually come from the Medinipur district to Kalighat in Calcutta, identify themselves as Hindus (Jain, 1999: 49). On the other hand, many paṭuās from other regions follow the Muslim faith. But the social customs that the paṭuās follow are derived from both Hindu and Muslim communities.

The paṭuās whose work is represented here are from the Medinipur district of West Bengal. They live in several villages of that district but most of those I met came from Habichak village. Some also came from Nanakpur and other villages but all were from East Medinipur. These painters identify themselves as belonging to the chitrakara jāti. They claim to belong neither to the Hindu nor to the Muslim religion and often the husband and wife take both Hindu and Muslim names. For instance, one of the painters from whom several paintings were acquired is Golap, who carries what is usually a Hindu name but whose wife has the Muslim name Nurjahan. Another couple who supplied me with many scrolls similarly had names spanning both religions: the husband was Niranjan, a Hindu name, and the wife was Jahanara, a Muslim name, but is also known as Jharna, which is usually a Hindu name. Other painters whose paintings have been collected as well are Tapan, Rahim, Khokan, Kalpana and Banku, whose names come from both Hindu and Muslim cultures. This practice of bestowing names across religions continues to be so common that within the same family one child is given a Hindu name and another a Muslim name. This may well be a strategic self-positioning for these families and individuals to deal with patrons across the religious divide in India. Sometimes the same person may bear two names, one Hindu and the other Muslim, using either, depending on the client (Singh, 2011: 65; Korom, 2006: 40).

Present-day paṭuās claim that from medieval times at the latest they have been painting stories from legends taken from the *Rāmayaṇa* and other sources, and have been singing the narratives while displaying their painted scrolls. Given the highly developed narrative patterns and stylistic idiom of present-day paṭas, this claim of an ancient and unbroken heritage does seem to be well-founded. Of the two epics, the *Rāmāyaṇa* and the *Mahābhārata*, the paṭuās draw subjects and stories mainly from the *Rāmāyaṇa* and relatively few from the *Mahābhārata*.

A large number of paintings also depict legends of Manasā Devī, the snake goddess, and other popular rural tales. But many paṭuās also deal with contemporary social and political themes, especially social injustice and the sufferings of the poor, that they observe or learn about across their own country as well as elsewhere in the world. In their work we may see the vigorous coexistence of tradition and modernity, which has been commented upon by art historians, a recent one being Pilar Jefferson (2014: 27–28). Viewing present reality through the lens of the legendary past, many of them depict the horrors of warfare by correlating modern conflicts with the devastating war in the *Rāmāyaṇa*.

Several paṭuās described their method of scroll painting to me at some length. They said that they collect twigs and various plants during the summer for four months, from March through June, around their villages and woods. During the monsoon, starting in July, they start making their own dyes by boiling plants and leaves and grinding various dry materials—burnt rice, rusty nails for black, brick for rusty brown and so on. They use leafy vegetables to extract greens and turmeric for yellow. After collecting the material, the family members get down to business in the monsoon and start painting different episodes from known stories that have been passed down to them through generations.

Paṭuās Today

In the past, the earlier generations of these painters used to divide their task among family members. Some members of the family would paint and others would sing and recite the stories. But now the division of labour is much less strict and often the same person paints, shows the scrolls and sings the descriptive songs. Holding on to their age-old performance format, they depict a story episode by episode, each in an individual frame and the whole comprising a complete scroll. The paṭuā unrolls one frame at a time and sings or recites a description of that frame, followed by the next frame. In the autumn, after the festival of Devī Durgā and through the winter, between October and February, usually the older family members come to the cities and sell the scrolls to buyers in their homes, some of whom are regular clients, including foreign scholars, or at the art fairs and book fairs that are held in cities in winter, such as the well-known book fair in Kolkata held in late January. Foreign scholars working on South Asia often visit India during this time, and they constitute a profitable market. Paṭuās take their business also to fairs at other cities. To my surprise, in the winter of 2015 I could not find any such scroll at Delhi Haat, a permanent bazar in Delhi with a large variety of folk art objects for sale, although I found a number of folk paintings from Orissa, Andhra and Madhubani, which were mostly treatments of religious and mythological episodes. Traditionally, the stories depicted and sung used to be drawn from mythology, but, with the passage of time, the narratives have changed to reflect contemporary social and political concerns and attitudes.

In the 1960s and 1970s, the Government of West Bengal began to encourage and promote the indigenous art forms of Bengal and to provide financial aid to artists, as governments elsewhere in India were doing to support folk arts and crafts. There was also a gradual shift to represent contemporary social, local and political issues and events. Government officials employed folk arts by commissioning artists to include public education issues such as family planning and drug abuse. Politics has provided material as well, including contemporary world affairs such as the Iraq War and George W. Bush's role in it as well as Osama Bin Laden's attack on the twin towers of New York. Social injustice and religious disharmony in India have also left a deep impact on the artists who paint scrolls and make up songs conveying anti-dowry and communal harmony messages. Recent cases of murder and rape in India have also attracted the attention of these rural artists. Paṭas have, thus, had a role in raising social and political awareness of socially and educationally disadvantaged people, especially in rural areas. These changes, however, have not displaced traditional paintings, their themes or their presentation format. To take the example of the subject of the present study, the tradition of painting episodes from the *Rāmāyaṇa* remains vigorous both in its popularity and its ethical attitude and content. In depicting *Rāmāyaṇa* episodes the paṭuās follow the 15th-century Bengali *Rāmāyaṇa* of Kṛttivāsa, though occasionally with local variations and additions.

As we go through the paṭas gathered in the present volume, it becomes evident that the pictorial *Rāmāyaṇa* that emerges offers a distinct narrative formed by the paṭuās through generations by means of their selection of episodes and artistic emphasis. The narrative may often deviate from the standard one familiar to most readers of the *Rāmāyaṇa,* but it is distinct to the art of the Bengal paṭas. Their individuality, however, consists not only in the matter of the narratives but also in their interpretive leanings. While the paṭuās take for granted that Rāma is indeed the noblest of mankind, indeed the god Viṣṇu in human form, and represent the rākṣasas as demons with all the insignia of evil in their portraiture, the dominant note of the pictorial form and the oral narration of the frames is not one of jubilation at the triumph of right over wrong. Rather, the paṭas convey a sense of pity at the pain inherent in disasters such as Rāma's exile, Sītā's abduction, Jaṭāyu's death, and, most insistently, Sītā's banishment and death. It is thus that the paṭas claim an individual place in Indian art as much by their form as by their emotional suggestiveness, as should be evident from the paṭas reproduced in this volume.

SONGS OF THE PAṬUĀS

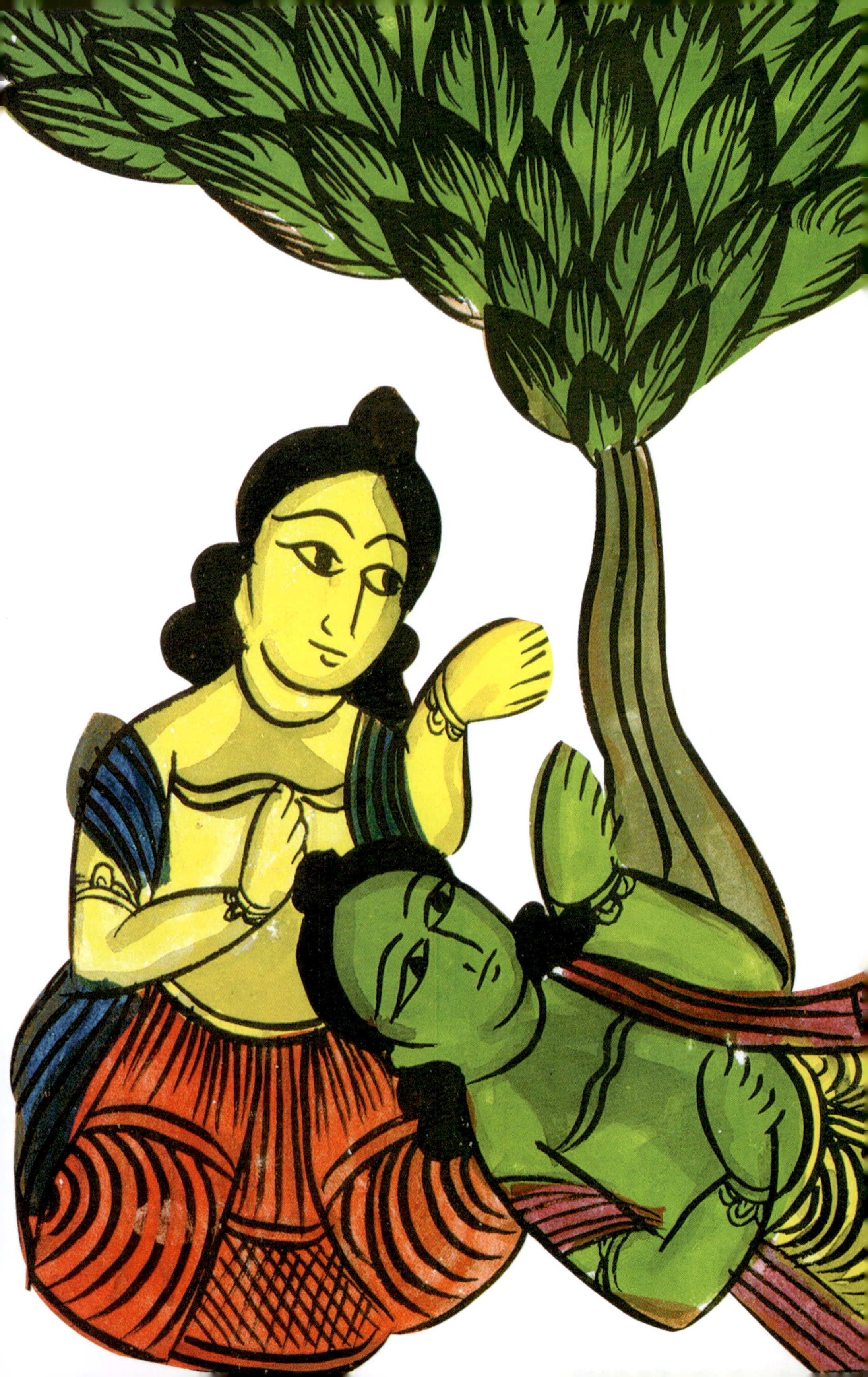

In studying and enjoying the paṭa as an art form it is important to bear in mind that it is a performing art and a public one at that. The work of paṭuās has never been a solitary artistic endeavour restricted to selected viewers and patrons; from the earliest time it has been aimed at the widest available audience, as suggested by the evidence of Bāṇabhaṭṭa's *Harṣacarita*, Canto 5 (Bāṇabhaṭṭa, 1985: 297). The traditional mode of presenting paṭas to the world has been and continues to be that of public display accompanied by the oral exposition of their subject-matter, which takes a ballad-like recitative form sung to some simple tune. The narrative unfolds before the viewer in a very literal sense as the painter unrolls the paṭa and sings the comment on the frame that appears. The subject of the narratives presented in the paintings and its visual representation being traditional rather than individual; the painter-singer follows a script familiar to the audience. The identity of the composer is not always known, but sometimes the paṭuā himself has written the script, as in the first example I offer here. Often the paṭuā chooses to recite a known text as accompaniment, such as passages from Kṛttivāsa. However, as a performing artist playing to a live audience and singing the verses as commentary on the particular frames on display, the painter does have the latitude of leaving out parts of whatever script he or she follows or moving lines ahead or back, in order that the song may keep close to the sequence and subject of the frames being displayed. Thus, even within the narrow boundaries set by the traditional legends portrayed, the painter's exposition of the images may reflect personal readings. Such individualism is found more in paṭas that depict modern subjects than those that follow ancient narratives such as the *Rāmāyaṇa*. When Niranjan Chitrakar of Habichak village showed me his paṭa depicting the Iraq War, he concluded his song with the lament that while Rāma could bring his dead soldiers back to life after the battle with Rāvaṇa, President Bush had no such power. The same paṭuā refrained from such personal observations when he composed songs to go with his *Rāmāyaṇa* paṭas, as my first specimen here shows, for paṭuās do not deviate from the storyline of traditional narratives that have been handed down by their forefathers. However, their diction, style of delivery and voicing does express the emotional implication of the scene being displayed, of which a persuasive example is Niranjan Chitrakar's song accompanying his paṭas of Sītā's abduction, which brings out the pathos of Sītā's predicament. Taking note of such songs, therefore, adds to our understanding of the paṭas as a composite and complex art form, as will be evident from the songs reproduced below, few though they are.

Of the compositions presented here, the first and the longest is by Niranjan Chitrakar from whom I collected two songs in the late 1990s. Only one is reproduced here because it is his original work, while the second, which recounts Sītā's descent into the earth, is not Niranjan's own composition but Kṛttivāsa's. I have therefore judged it superfluous for inclusion here. The second and very short song presented here is by Dukhyshyam Chitrakar and is part of Professor Frank Korom's collection. For the sake of comparison across folk performance genres that differ in form but relate the same narrative, I have added a *Rāmāyaṇa* song from a different tradition, namely, the musical form known as Bhādu found in parts of South Bengal.

Despite their difference in form and extent, it is clear that the three compositions presented here draw upon the same body of *Rāmāyaṇa* episodes and follow the same sequence of events, which is Kṛttivāsa's version of the epic. Beyond that version, however, there are tales existing in folk narrative traditions that offer perspectives on incidents and characters that widely vary from the tales depicted and sung by the paṭuās. One such tale, about Rāma's mother Kauśalyā, is presented here to provide a sense of that variation.

1. THE WEDDING OF RĀMA AND SĪTĀ, RĀMA'S EXILE, AND THE ABDUCTION OF SĪTĀ

The following composition sung by Nirajan Chitrakar encapsulates a long series of events comprising Rāma's wedding, his subsequent exile and the abduction of Sītā. It is reproduced here in Bengali transliteration exactly as sung, complete with one or two mispronounced words, followed by my English translation in prose.

Niranjan Paṭuā's song:

Biye holo Rāmcandra holen adhibās ǀ
Pitṛsatya pālite Rām yān banabās ǁ1ǁ
Āge cale Rāmcandra paścāte Jānakī ǀ
Tāhār paścāte calen Lakṣmaṇ dhnukī ǁ2ǁ
Upare rabir tāp nice tāt bāli ǀ
Calite nā pāre Sītā nanīr putalī ǁ3ǁ
Bhāṅgila tarur ḍāl Lakṣmaṇ dhare śire ǀ
Eri abachāyāy Lakṣmī calen dhīre dhīre ǁ4ǁ
Pañcabaṭīr bane Rām tulila hāwalī ǀ
Rām Sītā raichen base, Lakṣmaṇ praharī ǁ5ǁ
Śūrpaṇakhā elo ekdin Pañcabaṭīr bane ǀ

Nāk kān kāṭila tār ṭhākur Lakṣmaṇe ||6||
Nāk hāte kare rāṅḍī Laṅkāpure yāy |
Āchāḍ kheye paḍlo giyā Rāvaṇer pāy ||7||
Bṛddha rājā Daśānan kinā buddhi karila |
Bhagnīr durdaśā dekhi sarvāṅga jvalila ||8||
Sarvāṅga jvaliyā Rāvaṇ agnisama dhāy |
Mārīcke dhariyā Rāvaṇ mṛgayā sājāy ||9||
Ati chande nāce mṛga dekhite sundar |
Binay karye Jānakī bolche, Raghuvar ||10||
Mṛgaṭi dāogo dhare sukhī karo more |
Duḥkha tāp nibāriba mṛgaṭi dekhi re ||11||
Thāka re bhāi prāṇer Lakṣmaṇ nā sahe parāṇe |
Mṛga dharte yāba āmi Sītāra bacane ||12||
Yatakṣaṇ nā āsi āmi kuṭire phiriyā |
Sītāre rākhibe bhāi lakṣa ye kariyā ||13||
Eto bole Śrī Rāmcandra mṛga dharibāre |
Dhar dhar mār mār bole Rām tāḍiye niye gelo ||14||
Kichu dūre giyā Rām mṛgare badhilo |
Lakṣmaṇ Lakṣmaṇ bole mṛga ḍākite lāgilo ||15||
Kothā ācha prāṇera Lakṣmaṇ deha daraśan |
E bipade dekhā diye rākha go jīban ||16||
Ei ārtanād sur Sītār kānete gelo |
Lakṣmaṇe ḍākiyā Sītā kahite lāgilo ||17||
Śīghra eso debar Lakṣmaṇ tāmbul dhara khābe |
Tomār dādār anveṣaṇe daṇḍak bane yābe ||18||
Āmāy rekhe gelo Lakṣmī tomāy dekhibāre |
Tumi ābār yete balo dādāy dekhibāre? ||19||
Jānlām ogo debar Lakṣmaṇ jānlām tomār mati |
Rāmcandra marile habe āmār saṅgati ||20||
Viṣṇu Viṣṇu bale Lakṣmaṇ karṇe diyā hāt |
Tumi mātā Sumitrā mor pitā Raghunāth ||21||

Eso go mā ṛsir kanyā, satya karo āge ।
Gaṇḍīr ākār diye yābo kuṅḍyāte beḍiye ।।22।।
Gaṇḍīr ākār bāir hoile dekhchi yār mukh ।
Tribhuban ṭalāye yābe paśćāte pābi dukh ।।23।
Gaṇḍīr ākār diyā Lakṣmaṇ karilo gaman ।
Baṭabṛkṣatalā hote berolo Rāvaṇ ।।24।।
Bhikṣā dāo mā Jānakī bāḍī phire yāi ।
Tomār prabhur bāṇ ke baḍai ḍarāi ।।25।।
Bhikṣā nā pāiyā yugī maribāre chāy ।
Puruṣh hatyā mahāpāp Sītā ye ḍarāy।। 26।।
Kāñcaner thālkhāni ratnabharā kari ।
Yogī thāmāte bhikṣā dilo Jānakī jhiyārī ।।27।।
Gaṇḍīr bāhire bhikṣā dite bāire gelo ।
Dhariyā Sītār hāt rathe tule nilo ।।28।।
Kāṅdite kāṅdite Sītā malin badan ।
Ekbār dekhā dāo debar Lakṣmaṇ ।। 29।।
Uḍite uḍite rath karila gaman ।
Dasarather bandhu Jaṭāyu dila daraśan ।।30।।
Rāvaṇer rathke Jaṭāyu āḍe gilechilo ।
Rāvaṇer saṅge Jaṭāyur yuddha ārambhilo ।।31।।
Yotraś kore balre Jaṭāyu satya kore bala ।
Mitrabadhū Sītā āche rathera bhitara ।।32।।
Mitrabadhūr kathā śune Jaṭāyu lajjita hoilo ।
Gilechilo rathkhāni ugāriyā dilo ।।33।।
Brahmaśel chāḍe bāṇ Rāvaṇ mārilo ।
Kāṭhādaśek jami niyā Jaṭāyu paḍilo ।।34।।
Madhur vacane Rāmcandra pakṣīr pāne cāy ।
Atul caraṇ duṭī dekhibāre pāy ।।35।।
Āmāy badhe laye gelo Rāmcandra tomār gharaṇī ।
Sītār uddhār āge kara giyā Rām Raghumaṇi ।।36।।
Pakṣīr mukhete Rāmcandra pāiyā samācār ।

Duḥkhita haiyā śoy Rām bṛkṣer talāy ||37||
Deśe railo mātā re bhāi deśe marlo pitā |
Vidhir vidhāne bane curi holo Sītā ||38||
Eto bole Rāmcandra dukhī holo mane |
Sītā laye rākhlo Rāvaṇ aśoker bane ||39||
Medinipur jelāy āmār Habichake ghar |
Sītāharaṇer paṭ śunāy Nirañjan citrakar ||40||

Translation:

Rāma is married with [all prescribed] rituals and [soon after], he goes to exile to fulfil his father's promise [to his stepmother Kaikeyī]. He leaves [for the forest] with his bow and arrow, followed by Jānakī (=Sītā) and also by Lakṣmaṇa. The sun is hot up in the sky as is the sand below. Sītā, a delicate doll (lit: a doll made of cream), can walk no longer. Lakṣmaṇa breaks a branch from a tree [to protect her from the sun] and covers her head and Goddess Lakṣmī (=Sītā) walks slowly under that shade. Rāma builds a hut in the Pañcavaṭī forest and Rāma and Sītā reside there with Lakṣmaṇa guarding them. One day, Śūrpanakhā [the rākṣasī], visits the woods of Pañcavaṭī [and makes advances towards the brothers] and Lakṣmaṇa cuts her nose and ear [as she approaches them]. That evil woman runs to the city of Laṅkā holding her nose and falls at the feet of her brother Rāvaṇa. The old ten-headed king makes a plan [to avenge this humiliation]. He was angry at his sister's distress. Acting out of burning anger, Rāvaṇa gets hold of Mārīca, a rākṣasa, and [commands him] to disguise himself as a golden deer [to lure Sītā]. Seeing the beautiful golden deer dancing rhythmically, Jānakī asks Raghuvara (=Rāma) for the deer. "Please bring me the deer to make me happy and let me forget my sorrow," Sītā pleads. Rāma says to Lakṣmaṇa, "I can't bear it any longer. I will go and catch the deer as Sītā asks. Please protect Sītā with care until I return to the hut." Having said that,

Rāmacandra quickly runs towards the deer and kills it. [As the deer is dying] it starts calling Lakṣmaṇa's name, saying, "Where are you my dear brother Lakṣmaṇa? Show me your face and save my life." Hearing this cry Sītā calls Lakṣmaṇa, and offering him betel leaf [as an honour to persuade him], she asks him to go to the Daṇḍaka forest in search of his elder brother. [Lakṣmaṇa says,] "I was appointed by my elder brother to protect you, Lakṣmī (=Sītā), but now you are asking me to go in search for him." [Sītā angrily responds,] "Now I know what is your plan. You would like to possess me when Rāmacandra is dead." Lakṣmaṇa covers his ears, exclaiming, "Viṣṇu, Viṣṇu! You are like my mother Sumitrā and Raghunāth (=Rāma) is like my father. Please promise me, O daughter of a sage [that you will not cross the circle I am drawing around the hut]. As soon as you cross the line around the hut you will see a face and your entire world will change, and later it will bring grief and sorrow." Having drawn the circle around the hut, Lakṣmaṇa leaves and Rāvaṇa comes out immediately from behind the banyan tree [saying], "Give me alms Jānakī (=Sītā) and let me go home. I am afraid of your husband's arrow." Having received no alms, the Yogī [Rāvaṇa in disguise] looks around. Sītā worries about causing a man's death [by not giving alms], which would be a great sin. [Eventually] Jānakī fills a basket and crosses the line to give him alms and [Rāvaṇa] seizing her arms he puts her on his chariot. Sītā loses colour and wails, "O my brother-in-law, Lakṣmaṇa, show me your face once." But the chariot flies away. Jaṭāyu [the mythical bird], Daśaratha's friend, shows up and swallows Rāvaṇa's chariot sideways. Rāvaṇa and Jaṭāyu start fighting. Rāvaṇa tells Jaṭāyu that his

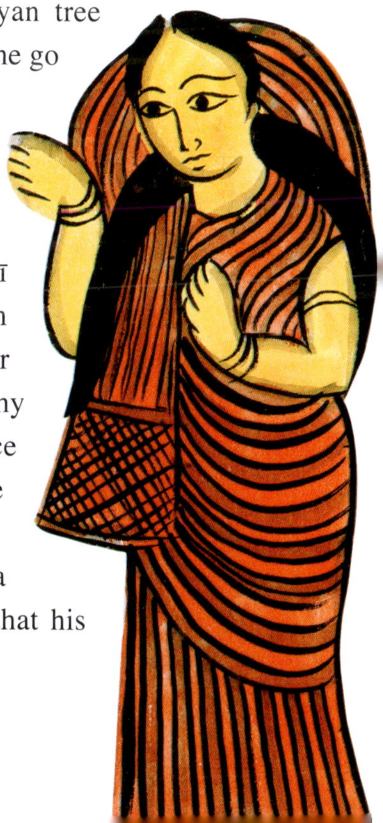

friend's daughter-in-law is on the chariot. Hearing this, Jaṭāyu feels ashamed and puts the chariot out of his mouth. Rāvaṇa shoots a Brahmaśela arrow and Jaṭāyu falls on the ground covering about ten kāṭhās of land. [Later, when Rāma sees him] he looks at the bird with compassionate eyes and talks to him in sweet words as the bird looks at Rāma's matchless [as a refuge for devotees] pair of feet. "O Raghumaṇi (=Rāma), [Rāvaṇa] took away your wife after striking me. Hurry and rescue Sītā." [When Rāma] hears this news from the bird he falls down under a tree. [Lamenting he says,] "My mother is back home and my father died there! Sītā has been abducted and this is my fate!" Rāmacandra is overcome with sorrow as he cries out in this manner. Meanwhile, after abducting Sītā, Rāvaṇa takes her to his kingdom Laṅkā and places Sītā in the Aśoka grove.

My home is in Habichak village in Medinipur. Niranjan Chitrakar is my name and I sing this song about Sītā's abduction.

2. A STORY FROM THE *RĀMĀYAṆA*

The following is a song sung by Dukhushyam Chitrakar, collected and translated by Frank J. Korom in the village of Naya in June 2002. He has very generously given me permission to share it. This is on Tāṭakāvadha, the killing of Tāṭakā; the lines reproduced here are exactly as I have received them.

A toddler in strength was Taraka [compared] to Rama,
Whose lines of arrows subdued the demon.
A single arrow moves in ten directions simultaneously,
One of which pierces the serpent Sheshnaga.
Another pierces a white crow,
[it] fell at the feet of Rama the great.
Humming the name of Rama, the crow
Left for its heavenly abode at Vaikuntha in a flower chariot.

The crow was none other than Ahalya, who turned to stone
As a punishment for the god's desire.

(Frank J. Korom's translation)

Professor Korom comments, "Unfortunately, neither Ahalya nor the white crow are shown in the scroll, since the emphasis is on Taraka, who gets two entire frames of six total." (Personal communication)

3. BHĀDU GĀN: A FOLK SONG ON THE RĀMA SAGA

The wide dissemination of Rāma tales among Bengali-speaking people has generated a variety of folk songs, many sung at social occasions such as weddings. The bhādu genre is from the bhādu festival prevalent in South Bengal in the month of Bhādra, the fifth month in the Bengali calendar, roughly late August to carly September, and the songs are frequently sung at weddings. The song below was collected by Madhusraba Dasgupta.

Rām yakhan pāñc bachure kuṣṭhi dekhe gaṇake ǀ
Hājār bachar paramāyu Rāmer, mṛtyu āche phāṅḍote ǀǀ1ǀǀ

When Rāma turns five, an astrologer checks his horoscope.
He may live for a thousand years [but] accidental death looms.

Aśok bane pātār kuḍo, Sītā pāsā khyāleche ǀ
Yagyir beśe Rāvaṇ ese Sītā hare liyeche ǀǀ2ǀǀ

In a leafy hut in the Aśoka grove, Sītā plays chess.
Rāvana comes in a sage's disguise and abducts her.

Sītā harye rāikhlā Rāvaṇ, rāikhlā Aśok bane ǀ
Dyākhbo, dyākhbo, sonār Laṅkā diyese dahan kare ǀǀ3ǀǀ

After abducting Sītā, Rāvaṇa keeps her in the Aśoka grove.
We shall see how that golden Laṅkā is burnt [to ashes]!

4. A CONTRARY VIEW OF KAUŚALYĀ IN BENGALI AND BHOJPURĪ FOLK SONGS

At a conference organised by Jadavpur University in Calcutta in early February of 2015, I heard Kabir Suman, a well-known singer from West Bengal, sing a Bengali folk song about the fate of a doe. A month later in Varanasi, Professor Archana Kumar of Benaras Hindu University repeated the same song but in the Bhojpuri language. Unfortunately, I could neither record the song nor get its exact text but the theme is the same in both the songs. Thus goes the story:

One morning, Queen Kauśalyā was sitting in her palace courtyard when a doe approached her with tearful eyes begging for her husband's hide, which King Daśaratha had killed on a hunting trip and presented to Kauśalyā. The doe begged for it, to keep it as a memento of her husband. Kauśalyā laughed and refused her request, saying that she was keeping the deer hide to make a toy-drum for her son Rāma to play with. She was not going to give it away to the doe and harshly drove her away.

This unusual story attributes an unexpected cruelty to Rāma's mother Kauśalyā, whose standard depiction in all *Rāmāyaṇas* is that of an epitome of motherly love and womanly tenderness. I have not come across this story or anything similar to it in any of the versions of the *Rāmāyaṇa* from which paṭuās draw their narratives. That this tale countervails and indeed subverts the idealisation of motherly tenderness in the *Rāmāyaṇa* is obvious. Equally obvious is that incidents of such discredit to the idealised characters in the *Rāmāyaṇa* have no place in the scheme of narratives, painted and sung, pursued by the paṭuās I have encountered.

THE RĀMĀYAṆA OF THE BENGALI PAṬUĀS

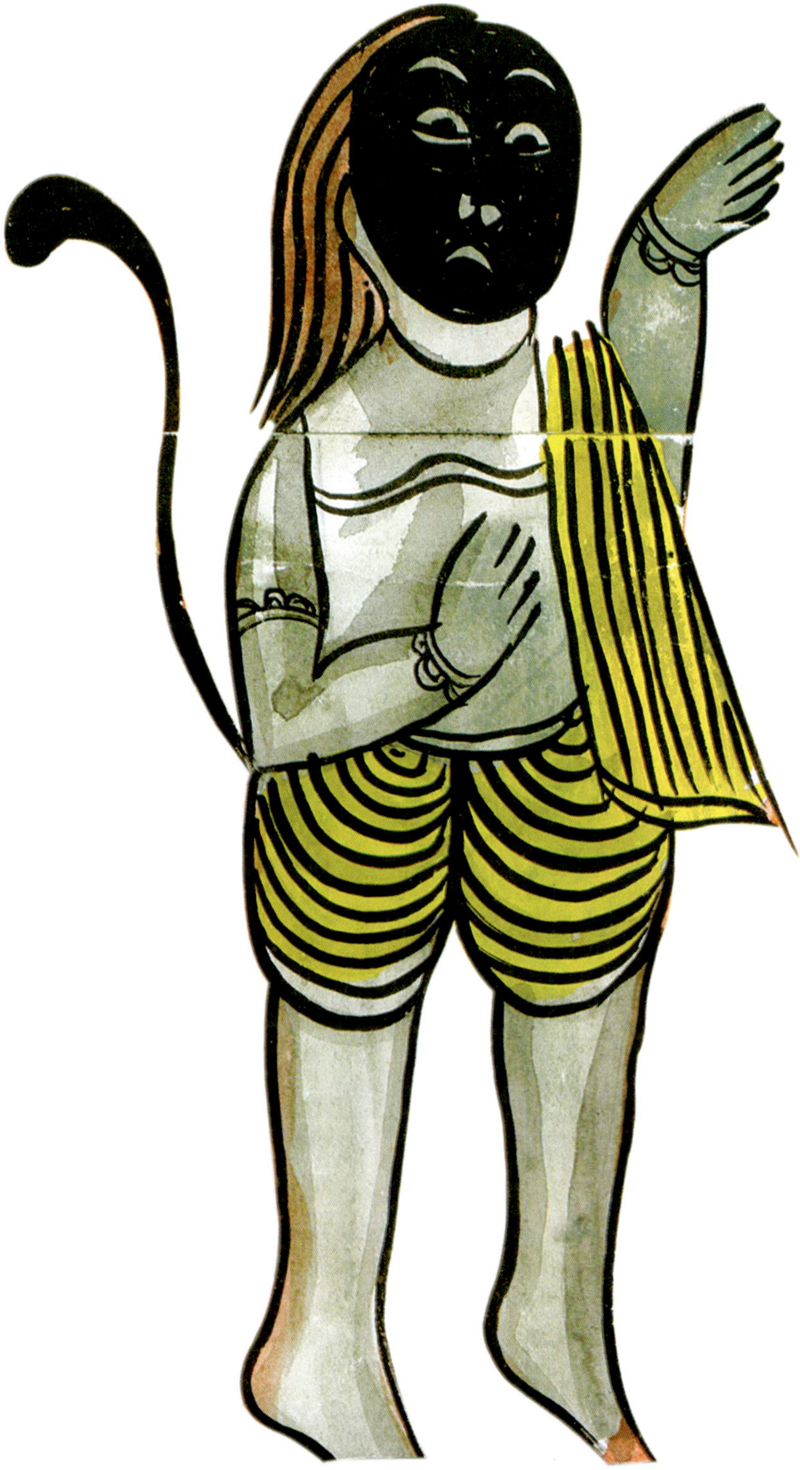

The *Rāmāyaṇa* paṭas presented in this volume were collected from a number of paṭuās, mostly from Habichak village and also a few other villages in the eastern Medinipur district of West Bengal. Given that more than one painter's work is represented here, each of whom lays out the story of the epic in his or her own way, I have attempted to present a coherent whole by culling individual frames from the paṭas and organising them into a clearly unfolding narrative or correlated images. Although Kṛttivāsa's Bengali *Rāmāyaṇa* has heavily influenced these painters, their story begins differently from Kṛttivāsa's. Since their focus is on what leads to Rāma's birth, they begin their pictorial narrative with the episode of Sindhuvadha or the killing of Sindhu by Daśaratha.[1] This seems to be the pattern for the paṭuās of Bengal when they paint *Rāmāyaṇa* scrolls; Sindhuvadha continues to be of prime importance to them, as evidenced by the large number of paṭas on the episode in all collections. Paṭuās are not concerned with the ancestral history of Rāma's family prior to Daśaratha. Placing the story in the context of family lineage or the divine plan for Rāma's birth has thus been ignored. In contrast, Kṛttivāsa devotes 29 sections to the history of generations prior to Daśaratha, going back even farther

1 Though the episode is present in other *Rāmāyaṇas*, the names of the father and the son are different there. Sindhu and Andhaka muni are Kṛttivāsa's creations (Bose, 2015: 234–40).

to begin with the divine plan behind the necessity for Rāma's birth on earth before launching the episode leading to Rāma's birth—the killing of Sindhu. I have not come across any scroll that begins the *Rāmāyaṇa* with any other matter preceding the Sindhu episode, nor have other collectors of paṭas I have consulted.

As already mentioned, this is not unique to the present collection and it seems that the paṭuās from all over Bengal are fascinated with Daśaratha's killing of Sindhu and skip the earlier part leading to Rāma's birth. Rāma's divinity was already established in the popular mind by the time depictions of the *Rāmāyaṇa* became part of the repertoire of these folk painters, for whom Lord Rāma, Viṣṇu in human form, became the focus of painting. Beginning with the history of Rāma's birth, paṭuās from Birbhum, for instance, begin their Rāma story with this episode and go on to follow the seven-part narrative scheme of Kṛttivāsa's (and Vālmīki's) text, focusing on four major clusters of events:

1) Sindhuvadha.
2) Rāma's birth and life until his marriage.
3) Rāma's exile, the abduction of Sītā and the killing of Rāvana.
4) The banishment of Sītā.

The Birbhum paṭuās base their paintings and their narration on these events (Bandyopadhyay, 1972: 1). Medinipur artists do the same, though their style of painting is distinctly different. Oddly enough, the paṭuās leave out one of the most dramatic phases of the early part of the action of the *Rāmāyaṇa*, comprising the joyous preparations for Rāma's coronation, Mantharā's wicked counsel to Kaikeyī, which leads to her demand for Rāma's exile to secure the throne for her son Bharata, and Daśaratha's death from a broken heart. These have never been subjects for any paṭuā's work, judging by the work of the painters encountered while gathering these paṭas. These episodes, found in the Ayodhyākāṇḍa section of written *Rāmāyaṇas* are not depicted in any paṭa I possess or have seen. This is also the experience of Professor Geraldine Forbes who has a large collection of paṭas. Professor Frank Korom has mentioned that in the course of singing and reciting the matter of their paṭas, the paṭuās add more episodes relating to the painted scrolls even though they are not actually represented. So while they may include in their songs passages about Kaikeyī, Mantharā or Daśaratha's death, they do not paint the episodes relating to them, nor do their paintings always correspond to what they sing. This has been my experience as well.[2]

The episodes from the *Rāmāyaṇa* included here represent the work of the paṭuās of the Medinipur district of West Bengal in my collection and set out to follow the progression of their storyline, which they claim has guided them for generations. In some of the kāṇḍas of Kṛttivāsa's *Rāmāyaṇa* (*KR*) the entire epic is condensed into a few lines. In the last but one section of Kiṣkindhyākāṇḍa, Hanumān tells Sampāti the story of the *Rāmāyaṇa* in eight lines:

Ādyakāṇḍe Rāmajanma vivāha Sītār/
Ayodhyāy vanavās tyāji rājyabhār//
Āraṇyakāṇḍete Sītā hare durāśay/
Kiṣkindhyāy Vālivadh kaṭak sañcay//
Sundarākāṇḍete setubandha camatkār/
Laṅkākāṇḍe Rāvaṇer savaṁśe saṁhār//
Kathā sātkāṇder uttarākāṇḍe paḍe/
Gāila uttarākāṇḍa Rāmāyaṇa niṅḍe//

Adikāṇda describes Rāma's birth and marriageI
Ayodhyākāṇḍa focuses on Rāma's abdication of throne and exileII

2 Personal communication with Geraldine Forbes and Frank J. Korom.

Āraṇyakāṇda follows the abduction of Sītā by the evil one।
Kiṣkindhyā describes the killing of Vāli and gathering of soldiers।
Sundarākāṇda narrates building of the wonderful bridge।
Laṅkākāṇḍa describes the killing of Rāvaṇa and his family।
Uttarākāṇda summarises the entire story।
Thus the Uttarākāṇda is the extract of the entire story॥
(*KR*, 1957: Kiṣkindhyākāṇda p. 198; my translation)

In the paṭas I have examined, the paṭuās follow the above storyline on the whole, except that Rāma's disinheritance is not shown in their paintings. To be noted is Kṛttivāsa's omission from the summary the banishment episode of Sītā in the Uttarākāṇḍa even though it is a crucial part of his own story; it is also a favourite subject for the paṭuās.[3] The six-part narrative of the paṭuās presented here unfolds through the sequence of the painted frames accompanying the text. Taken as a whole, this painted version of the *Rāmāyaṇa* draws—with the exception noted above—upon the seven kāṇḍas or books that comprise the major literary and oral *Rāmāyaṇas* of Bengal, successfully maintaining the flow of the story through four major areas of events.

Since the paṭas highlight only selected events from the epic's plot and do not cover the narrative between them, the action of each kāṇḍa or book of the epic has been summarised at the beginning of each. The plates presented here follow the sequence of kāṇḍas and are numbered by kāṇḍa, episode and frame number, thus: Ādi.i.1., and the description of each plate is followed by the artist's name. Provided within brackets and in italics will be found the narrative transition between the paṭa frames when the link is not specifically illustrated.

3 Also to be noted is that Kṛttivāsa calls the first kāṇḍa Ādikāṇḍa rather than Bālakāṇḍa as in Valmīki, and spells the titles of some of the kāṇḍas slightly differently from Valmīki, thus: Āraṇyakāṇḍa, Sundarākāṇḍa and Uttarākāṇḍa.

❄ The paṭuās and their locations

- Niranjan Chitrakar: Habichak village, East Medinipur, West Bengal.
- Kalpana Chitrakar (Niranjan's wife): Habichak village, East Medinipur, West Bengal.
- Golap Chitrakar: Habichak village, East Medinipur, West Bengal.
- Nurjahan Chitrakar (Golap's wife): Habichak village, East Medinipur, West Bengal.
- Khokan Chitrakar (Nurjahan's son): Habichak village, East Medinipur, West Bengal.
- Tapan Chitrakar: Nandapur village, East Medinipur, West Bengal.

BOOK I

ĀDIKĀṆḌA: THE BEGINNING

The story begins with the accidental killing of the young hermit Sindhu by Daśaratha, king of Ayodhyā, followed by the curse of Sindhu's father, the blind sage, that the king would similarly die of grief upon losing his son. The sage and his wife then die on the same pyre as their son. Daśaratha, who has never had a son, returns to Ayodhyā and informs his three queens that the curse will in fact bring about the birth of sons. A yajña is performed for this purpose and the queens bear four sons. This long kāṇḍa then goes on to relate Rāma's youthful prowess and his marriage to Sītā.

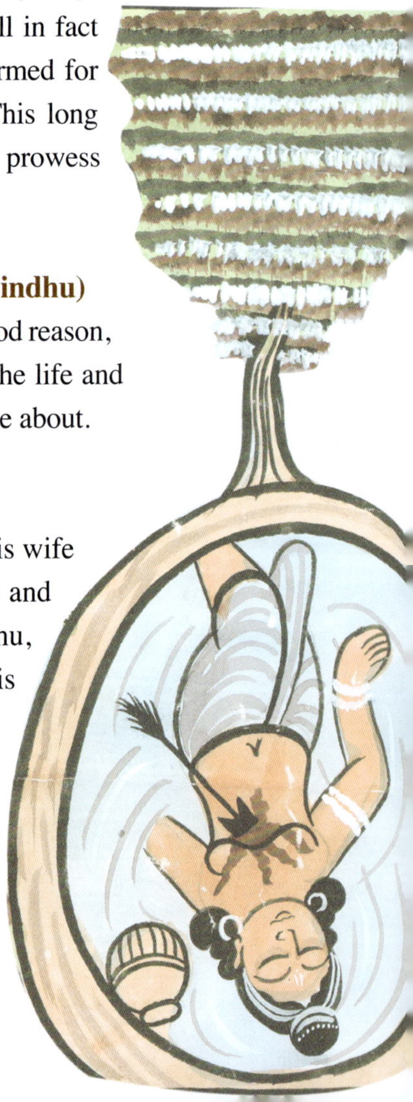

❈ Episode 1: Sindhuvadha (the killing of Sindhu)

This is a favourite subject of paṭuās, and with good reason, for it is this incident that initiates the story of the life and deeds of Rāma by explaining how his birth came about.

Ādi.i.1.

A sage named Andhaka lives in a forest with his wife and only child, a son called Sindhu. Both he and his wife are blind and looked after by Sindhu, who carries them around in two baskets on his shoulders. [Tapan Chitrakar]

Ādi.i.2.

Sindhu watches over his parents while they rest in their hut. [Tapan Chitrakar]

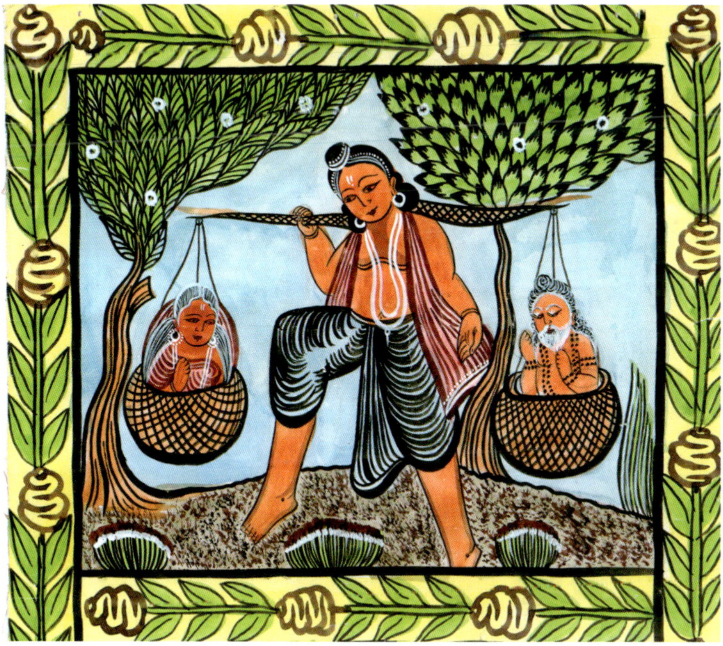

Ādi.i.1.

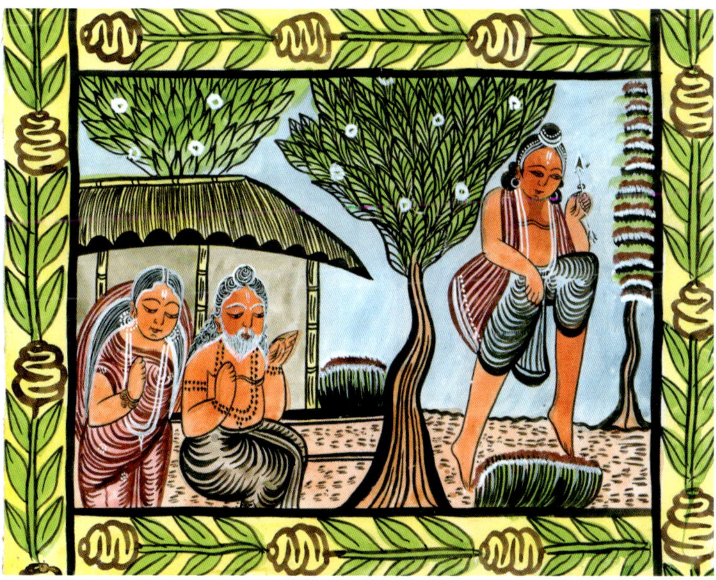

Ādi.i.2.

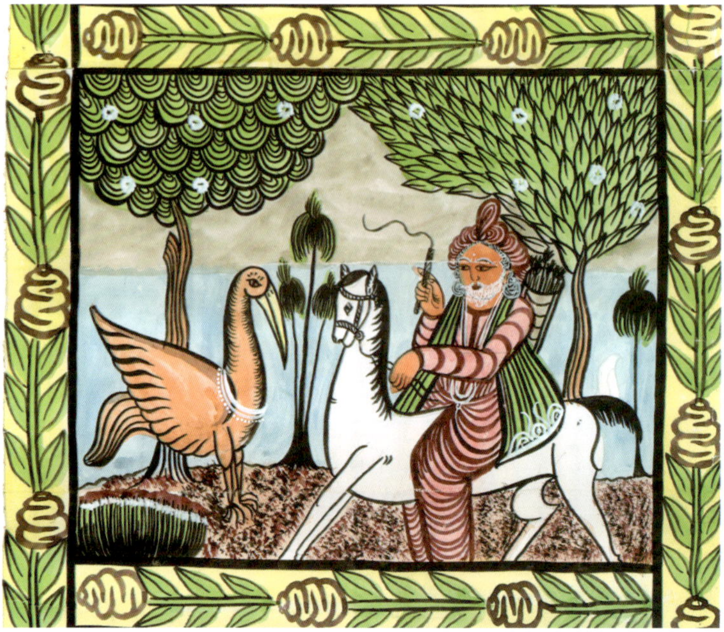

Ādi.i.3.

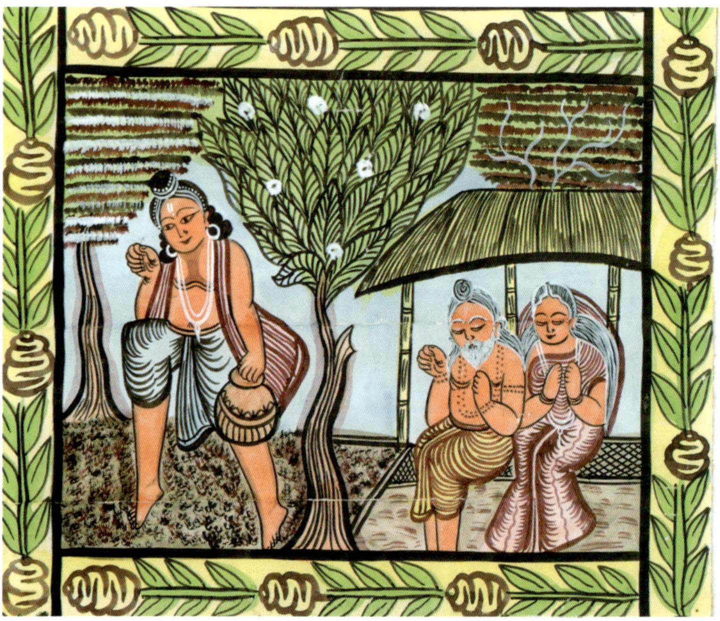

Ādi.i.4.

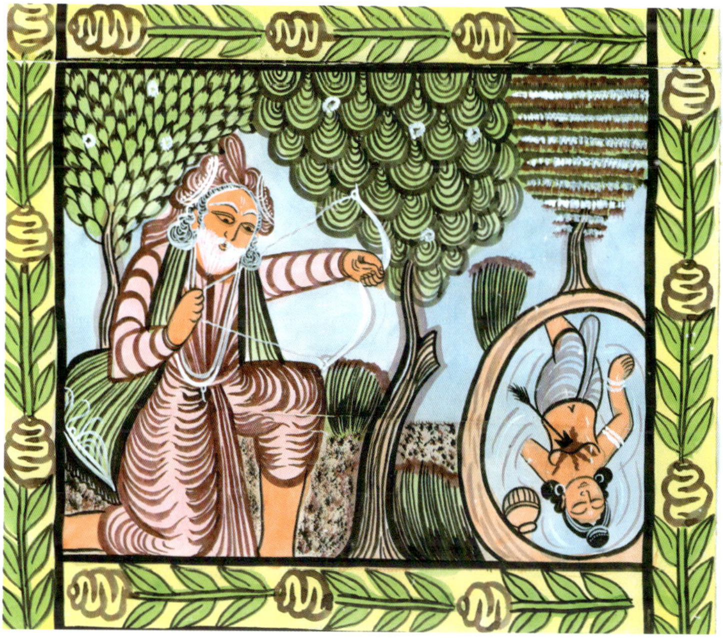

Ādi.i.5.

Ādi.i.3.

Daśaratha goes on a hunting trip to the forest where Sindhu lives with his parents. [Tapan Chitrakar]

Ādi.i.4.

One day, Sindhu goes to fetch water for his parents from a nearby river with a pitcher in his hand. The king reaches the same river at the same time. [Tapan Chitrakar]

Ādi.i.5.

[*As Sindhu is dipping his pitcher to fill it with water, the pitcher makes a gurgling sound, which Daśaratha mistakes for the sound of a deer drinking water from the river.*] Daśaratha shoots an arrow towards the sound of gurgling water to hunt the deer down. Instead, he shoots Sindhu who falls down and dies. [Tapan Chitrakar]

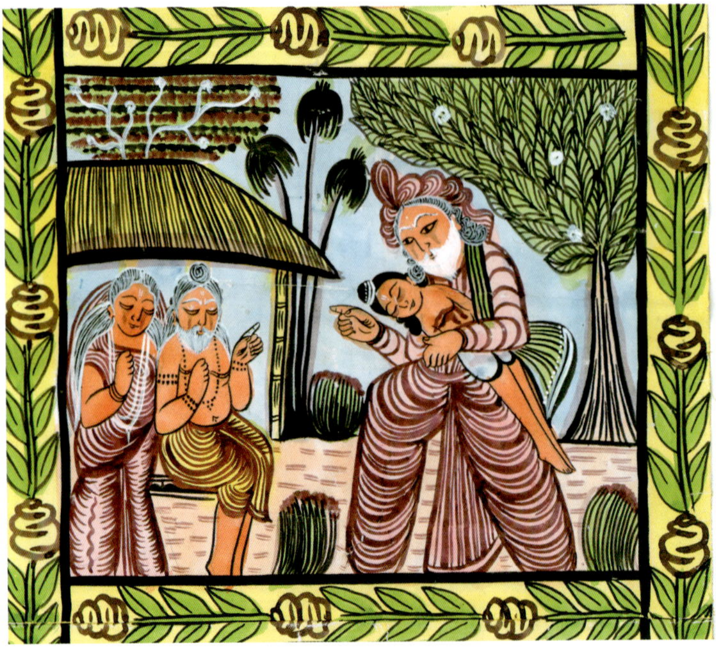

Ādi.i.6.

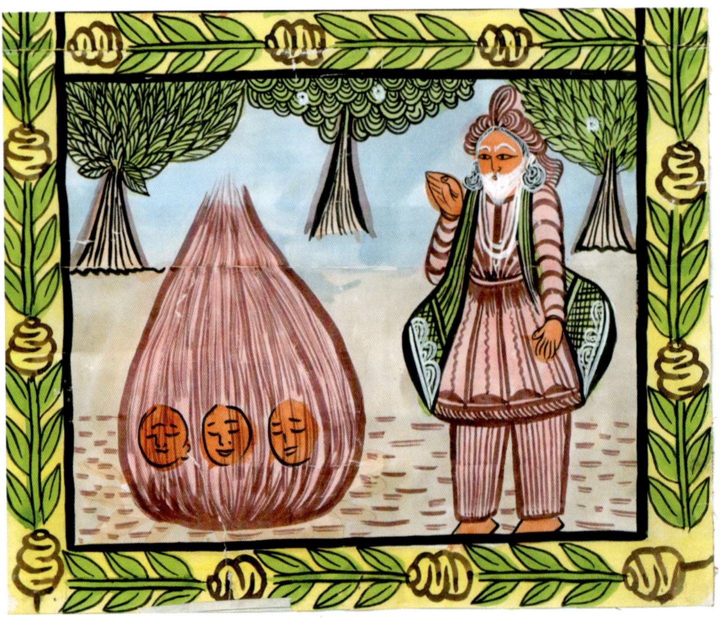

Ādi.i.7.

Ādi.i.6.

Realising his mistake, Daśaratha is remorseful. Picking up Sindhu's lifeless body, he walks towards the hut where the young man's parents live. Sindhu's parents are eagerly waiting for their son. Hearing footsteps, they call out his name. Instead, Daśaratha brings the body of their son and explains the terrible tragedy. The couple is overwhelmed with grief and tears roll down their cheeks. [Tapan Chitrakar]

Ādi.i.7.

The sage and his wife cannot live without their son and in his dying breath the sage curses the childless king [*that he will suffer similar śoka or grief at the loss of his son and die of putraśoka (lit: grief caused on account of a son). However, this curse becomes a boon in disguise for Daśaratha who is thus blessed with the promise of the birth of a son, which would be necessary for him to suffer the loss of a son.*] The king performs the ritual immolation for all three of his victims [*and returns to Ayodhyā.*]. [Tapan Chitrakar]

❈ Episode 2: The birth of Rāma

Daśaratha returns to Ayodhya and performs a ritual sacrifice which leads to the birth of four sons, Rāma and his three brothers.

Ādi.ii.1.

Daśaratha returns to his kingdom and tells his three queens—Kauśalyā, Kaikeyī and Sumitrā—about his experience during his hunting trip, which had resulted in the curse that would bring about the birth of a son/sons. [Khokan Chitrakar]

Ādi.ii.2.

Daśaratha holds a ritual sacrifice to plead for the birth of a son [putrakāmeṣṭi yajña], to perform which he has the young sage Ṛśyaśṛṅga

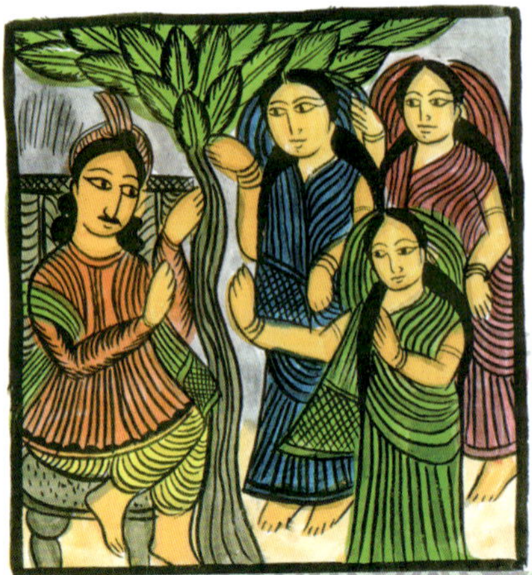

Ādi.ii.1.

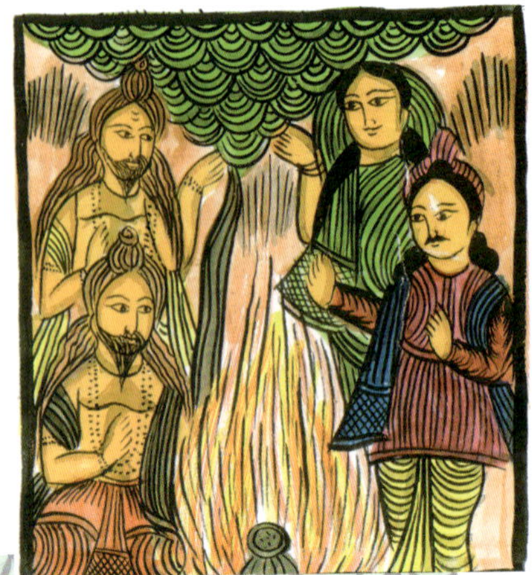

Ādi.ii.2.

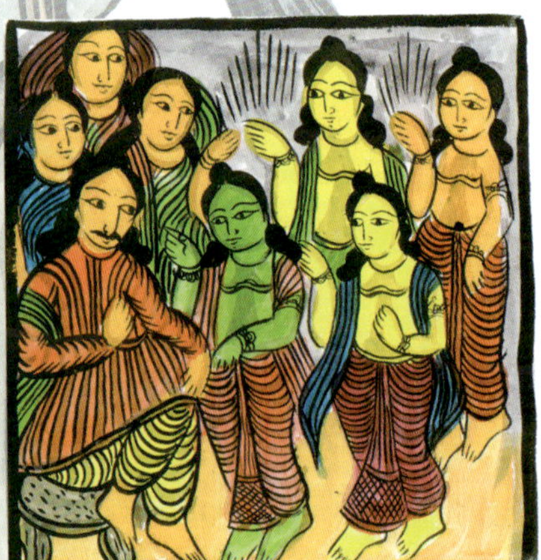

Ādi.ii.3.

brought in as advised by the family priest Vasiṣṭha. From the sacrificial fire the sage brings to the king a dish of sanctified caru (a milk pudding), which he then distributes to his queens. [Khokan Chitrakar]

Ādi.ii.3.

The three queens of Daśaratha share the caru, and after consuming it they become pregnant and give birth to four sons. Kauśalyā bears Rāma, Kaikeyī bears Bharata, and Sumitrā bears the twins, Lakṣmaṇa and Śatrughna. People rejoice all over the kingdom. [Khokan Chitrakar]

❄ Episode 3: Tāṭakāvadha (the killing of Tāṭakā)[4]

Rāma and Lakṣmaṇa journey to the forest with Sage Viśvāmitra to defend forest-dwelling hermits from marauding rākṣasas. They kill the female demon Tāṭakā, who had been terrorising the hermits of the forest.

Ādi.iii.1.

One day, Viśvāmitra [*the kṣatriya king who had become a Brahmin sage by practising rigorous tapas*] visits King Daśaratha and asks that Rāma and Lakṣmaṇa be sent with him to defend forest-dwelling sages and hermits against the depredations of rākṣasas or demons. Though reluctant to let his sons venture into danger, Daśaratha is persuaded by the

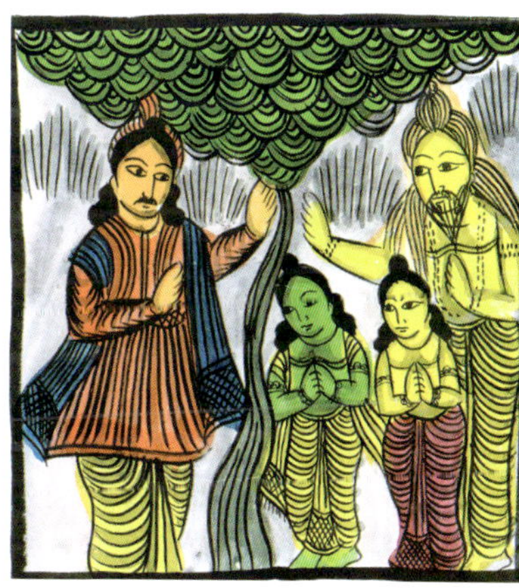

Ādi.iii.1.

4 For a song on Tāṭakāvadha, see above, "Songs of the Paṭuās" The song is by Dukhushyam Citrakar and goes with his paṭa of the episode, which is part of the large collection of Bengali *Rāmāyaṇa* paṭas collected by Frank J. Korom, who has very kindly permitted me to reproduce it.

family priest, Sage Vasiṣṭha, to let his two sons go with Viśvāmitra. [Khokan Chitrakar]

Ādi.iii.2.
Rāma and Lakṣmaṇa follow Viśvāmitra to the forest. [Khokan Chitrakar]

Ādi.iii.3.
They encounter the vicious demoness Tāṭakā, who attacks them. But Rāma kills Tāṭakā and brings peace to the forest. [Khokan Chitrakar]

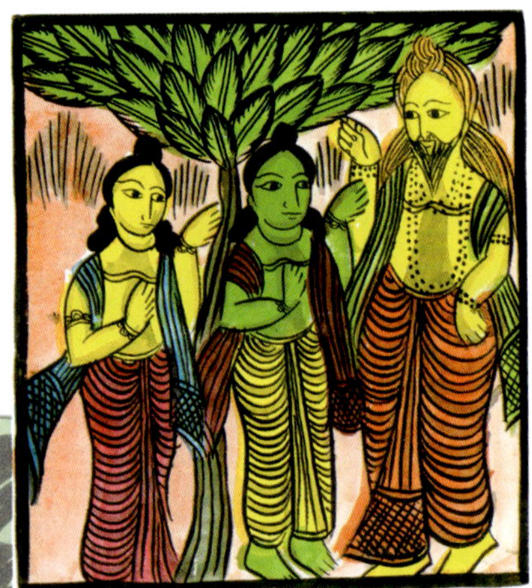

Ādi.iii.2.

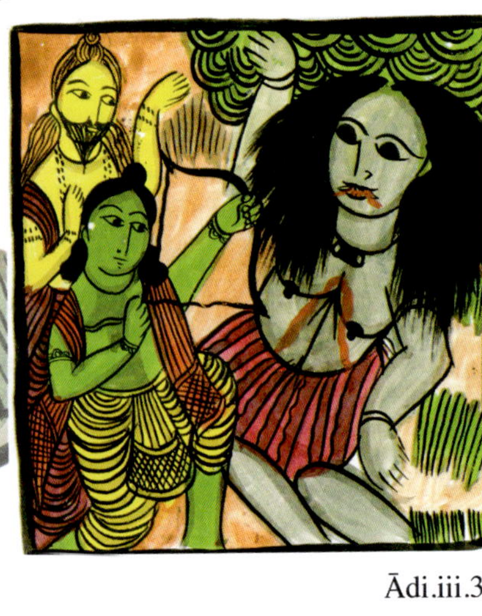

Ādi.iii.3.

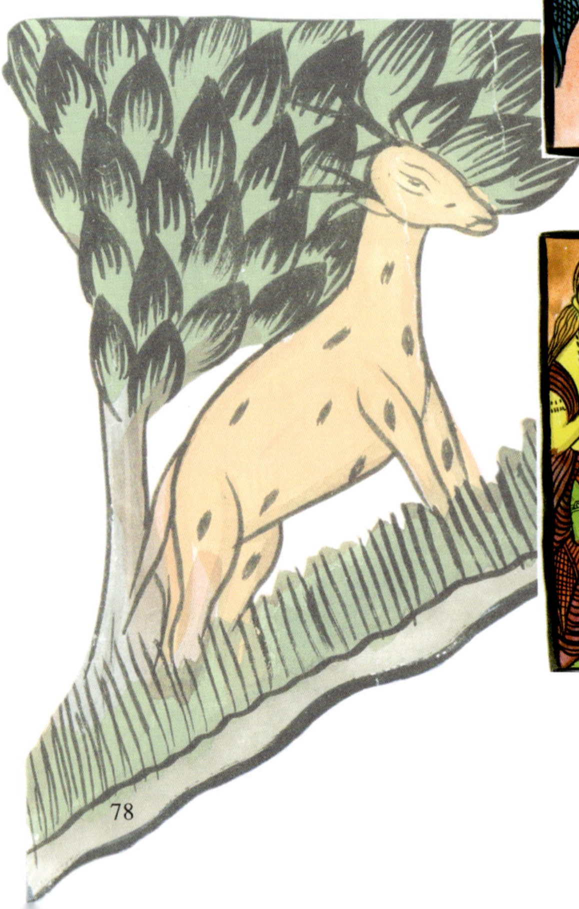

❄ Episode 4: The wedding of Rāma and Sītā:

After the killing of Tāṭakā, Viśvāmitra leads Rāma and Lakṣmaṇa to King Janaka's kingdom Mithilā, where Rāma wins Sītā.

Ādi.iv.1.

[*After they have subdued the rākṣasas in the forest, Rāma and Lakṣmaṇa are taken by Viśvāmitra to visit King Janaka, the ruler of Mithilā, to contend for the hand of his daughter Sītā in marriage. Sītā is to be won by lifting a special bow, the Haradhanu, which was a gift from Śiva or Hara, and of such great weight and tension that none of the many princes who had tried to fit a string to it had succeeded even to lift it.*] Rāma lifts the Haradhanu and in stringing it, he breaks it into two as Sītā watches. [Khokan Chitrakar]

Ādi.iv.2.

King Janaka gives his blessing to the union of Rāma and Sītā. [Khokan Chitrakar]

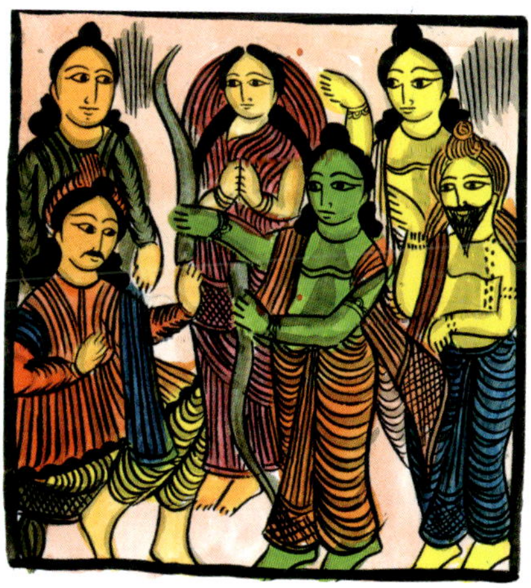

Ādi.iv.1.

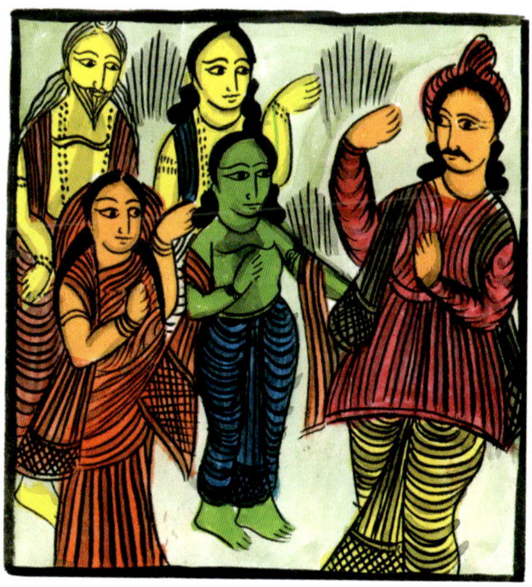

Ādi.iv.2.

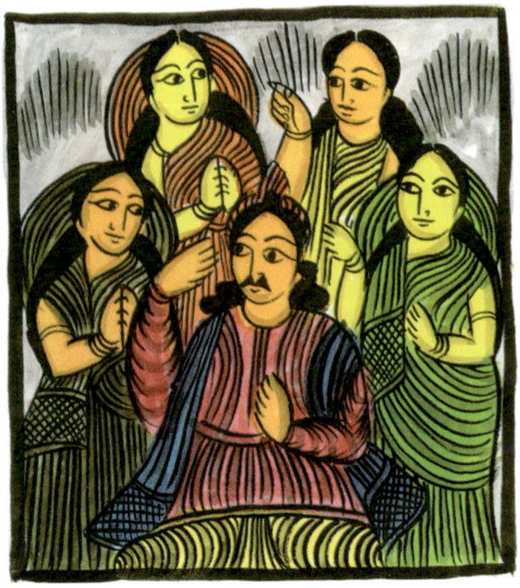

Ādi.iv.3.

Ādi.iv.3.

Janaka arranges the marriage of four princesses, Sītā to Rāma, his other daughter Urmilā to Lakṣmaṇa, and two other cousins of Sītā, Śrutakīrtī to Bharata and Māṇḍavī to Śatrughna. [Khokan Chitrakar]

[*After the weddings, Rāma and the rest of the party return to Ayodhyā.*]

Here ends the Ādikāṇḍa, the first book of the *Rāmāyaṇa*.

BOOK II

AYODHYĀKĀṆḌA: EVENTS IN AYODHYĀ

The second kāṇḍa is missing from the repertoire of the paṭuās whose paṭas I have collected. In all written versions of the *Rāmāyaṇa,* the story continues into this part with Daśaratha's return to Ayodhyā with his sons. Immediately afterwards, preparations for Rāma's coronation begin when Daśaratha decides to abdicate his throne and crown Rāma. But he cannot carry out this decision as Kaikeyī, the second queen of Daśaratha, is incited by her maid Mantharā to demand from him his long-deferred vow to give her whatever her wish might be. Her demands are that Rāma be exiled to the forest for 14 years and that in his place her own son Bharata be crowned. To help keep his father's vow, Rāma goes into exile, accompanied by Sītā and Lakṣmaṇa. Daśaratha dies of grief. Bharata returns from his maternal grandfather's home to find out what has happened during his absence. He refuses the throne and tries in vain to bring Rāma back to take the throne.

Inexplicably, I have found no paṭa depicting these episodes that comprise the Ayodhyākāṇḍa, whether by the paṭuās I have come across or by any others whose work my friends and colleagues know. No explanation seems plausible for bypassing such crucial and dramatic events as Kaikeyī's manipulation of Daśaratha or such iconic figures as Mantharā the evil hunchback. The omission seems even more puzzling when we note that Rāma's ready acceptance of exile has been traditionally held up as a model of filial duty and self-sacrifice within the ideology of public and private morality in India, and leaving it out in the pictorial tale unaccountably overlooks this important part of Rāma's moral reputation. That the paṭuās are not ignorant of the event of his disinheritance is evident from the songs they sing as they outline the narrative. Some of the songs I have collected refer to these episodes, thus bridging the gap in the paṭas. Two such songs, one from my collection, the other from Frank J. Korom's, are included in the chapter "Songs of the Paṭuās".

Whatever the reason may be for ignoring the cause of Rāma's departure for the forest, the paṭuās resume the tale as Rāma, Sītā and Lakṣmaṇa set out for the forest, their *banagamana* (journey to the forest) being one of the commonest subjects for paṭas. With this, the sequence of paṭas moves into the epic's next part, the Āraṇyakāṇḍa, which describes the forest sojourn of Rāma, Sītā and Lakṣmaṇa.

BOOK III

Āraṇyakāṇḍa: The Forest Sojourn

Rāma, Sītā and Lakṣmaṇa arrive at Citrakūta forest, where they live for a while before moving on to Daṇḍaka forest. In their wanderings they visit many hermitages and sages, eventually arriving at Pañcavaṭī forest where they settle down in a hut that Lakṣmaṇa builds. Here they meet their father's friend Jaṭāyu, a great bird warrior celebrated in myths.

Sometime later, they are visited by the demoness Śūrpanakhā, whose romantic advances they meet by cutting off her nose and ears. This leads to Sītā's abduction by Śūrpanakhā's brother Rāvaṇa, an episode termed Sītāharaṇa, which is one of the commonest subjects of paṭas, followed by Rāvaṇa's battle with Jaṭāyu, who is fatally wounded.

❄ Episode 1: Rāma, Sītā and Lakṣmaṇa in the forest

Rāma, Sītā and Lakṣmaṇa set out on foot for the forest, where they reside in a small hut. Their quiet life in exile is soon disturbed by the appearance of the rākṣasī Śūrpanakhā, the evil rākṣasa king Rāvaṇa's sister. When Lakṣmaṇa punishes her for making romantic overtures to the brothers by cutting off her nose and ears, she seeks help from Rāvaṇa to avenge herself.

Āraṇya.i.1.

Rāma, Sītā and Lakṣmaṇa leave for the forest, walking barefoot. Sītā's delicate feet are hurting in the scorching heat of the sun and she feels tired. Lakṣmaṇa breaks a branch from a tree to give her shade from the sun, as they walk on. [Niranjan Chitrakar]

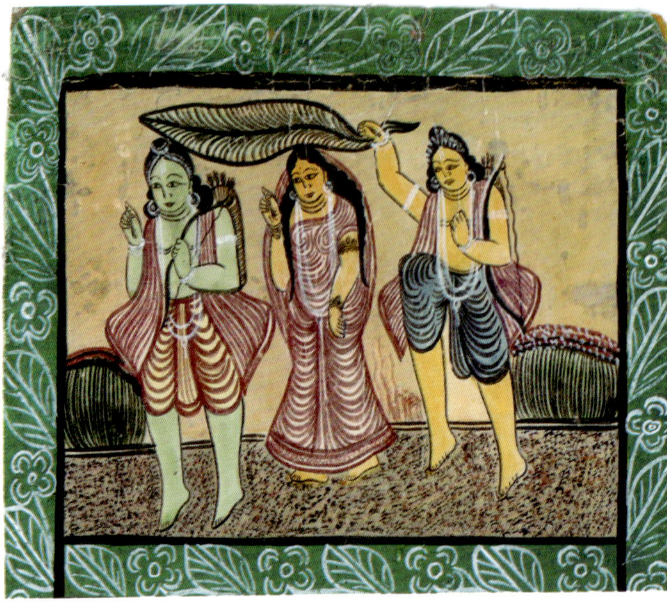

Āraṇya.i.1.

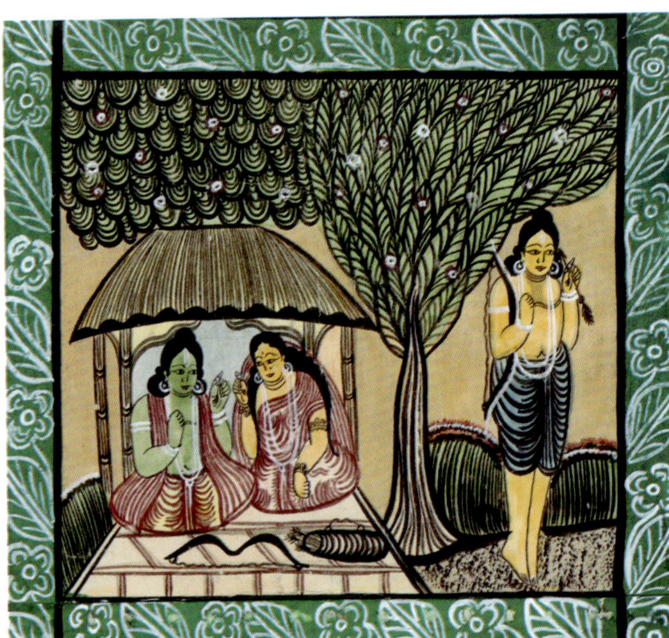

Āraṇya.i.2.

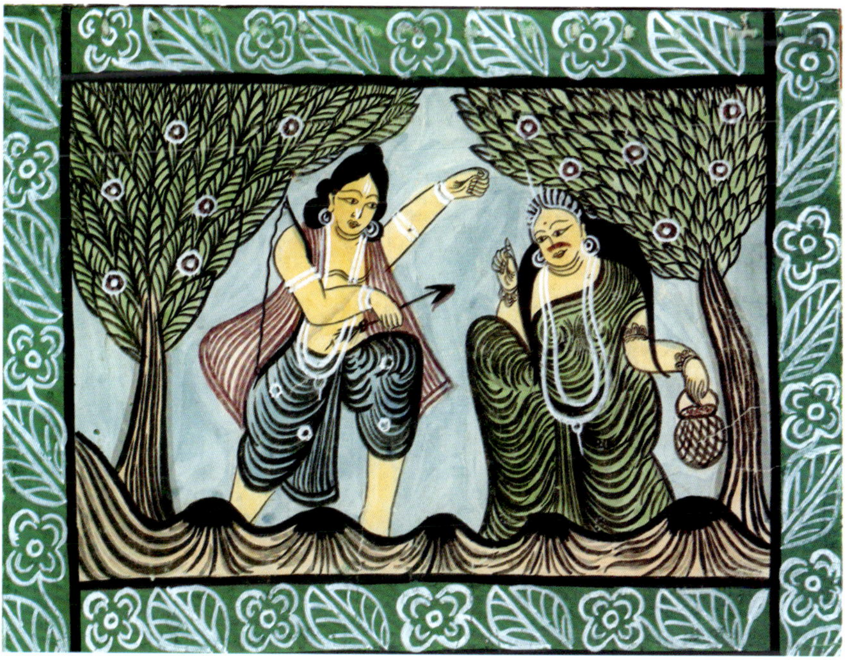

Āraṇya.i.3.

Āraṇya.i.2.
They reach a forest where Lakṣmaṇa builds a modest hut, in which Rāma and Sītā settle in while Lakṣmaṇa guards them. They enjoy a peaceful life for a brief period. [Niranjan Chitrakar]

Āraṇya.i.3.
That peace is soon destroyed. One day a demoness [rākṣasī] named Śūrpanakhā approaches Rāma in the form of a beautiful young woman and begs him to marry her. When Rāma refuses her she approaches Lakṣmaṇa, who not only repulses her but when she threatens Sītā as a rival he punishes her by cutting off her nose and ears. [Niranjan Chitrakar]

❄ Episode 2: Sītāharaṇa (the abduction of Sītā)

Furious at the humiliation of his sister, Rāvaṇa resolves to take revenge and commands the rākṣasa Mārīca, a shape-changer, to go to the same forest where Rāma, Sītā and Lakṣmaṇa live and tempt Sītā in the form of a golden deer. Rāma leaves to catch the deer and later Lakṣmaṇa goes to help him. In their absence Rāvaṇa, disguised as a mendicant, abducts Sītā.

Āraṇya.ii.1.

Śūrpanakhā flees to her brother Rāvaṇa, the rākṣasa king of Laṅkā, and reports her humiliation, showing him her dismembered nose streaming with blood. [To avenge her, Rāvaṇa commands Mārīca to go to the forest abode of Rāma and Sītā as a golden deer.] [Niranjan Chitrakar]

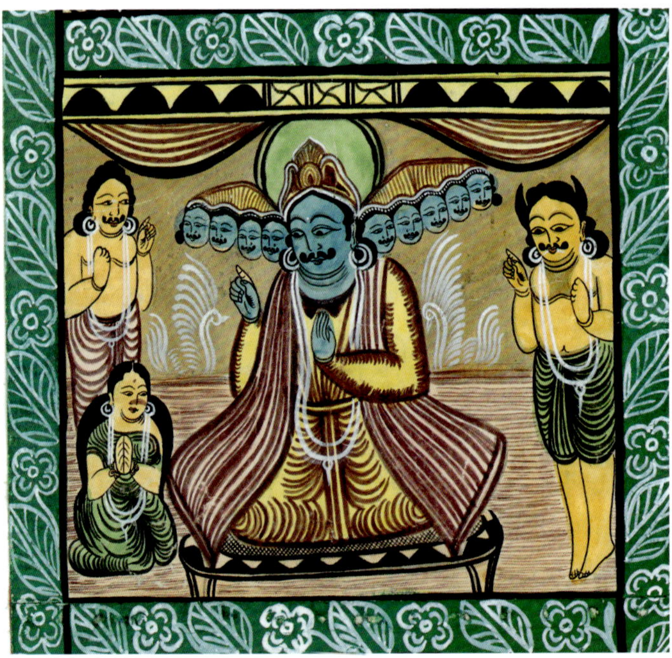

Āraṇya.ii.1.

Āraṇya.ii.2.

Mārīca the golden deer playfully gambols within Sītā's sight. Enchanted by the deer, Sītā begs Rāma to catch it for her [*to play with and eventually to take it back to Ayodhyā*]. [Niranjan Chitrakar]

Āraṇya.ii.3.

[*Rāma leaves Sītā to catch the deer, asking Lakṣmaṇa to guard her*.] Rāma shoots an arrow and kills the deer, which is actually the rākṣasa Mārīca. [*With his dying breath and in Rāma's voice Mārīca calls upon Lakṣmaṇa to come for help*.] [Niranjan Chitrakar]

Āraṇya.ii.4.

[*Lakṣmaṇa reluctantly leaves after drawing a protective circle around the hut and telling Sītā not to step outside the circle*.] Taking advantage

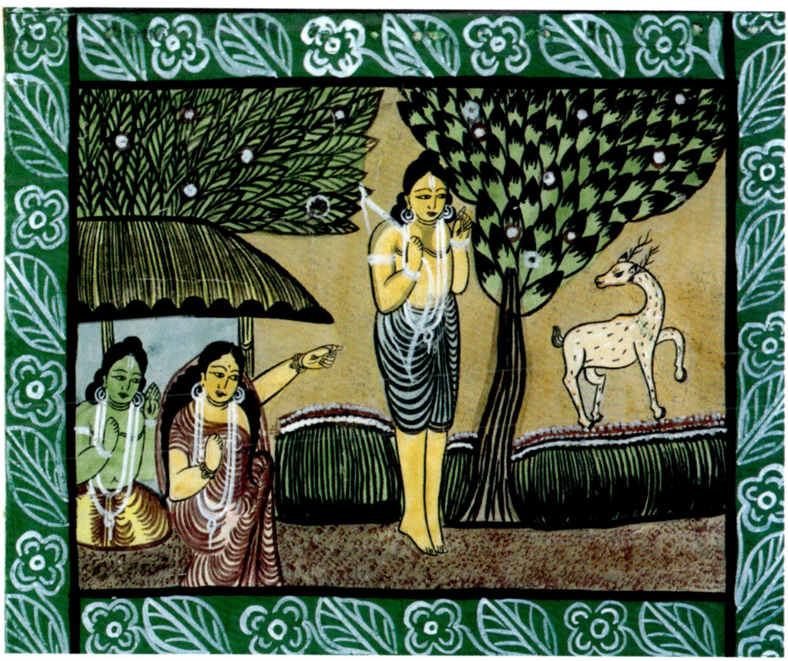

Āraṇya.ii.2.

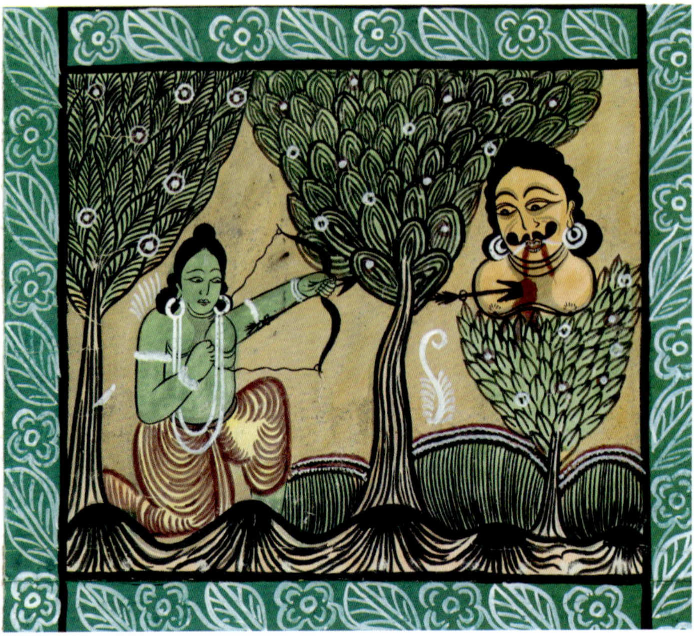

Āraṇya.ii.3.

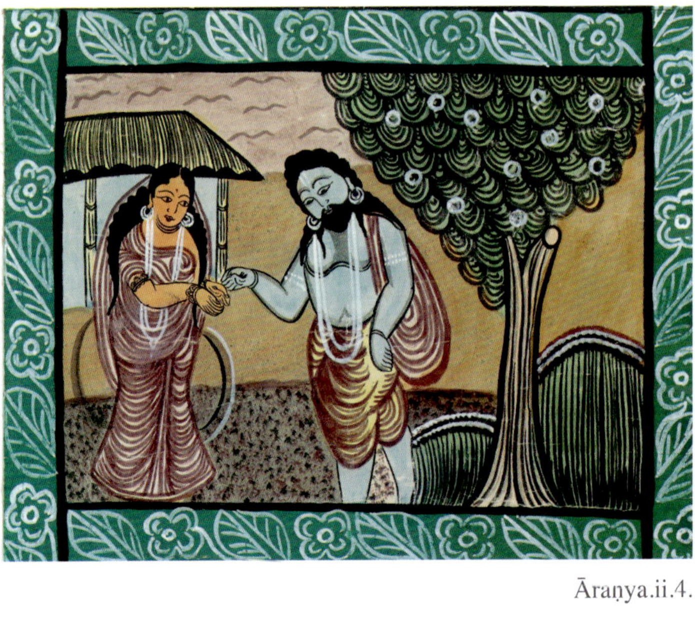

Āraṇya.ii.4.

of the men's absence, Rāvaṇa appears in a mendicant's disguise and asks Sītā for alms. [*Although reluctant, Sītā must obey the call of hospitality and thus unable to refuse the mendicant's plea, she crosses the protective line. Rāvaṇa at once seizes her and flies for his kingdom on his aerial chariot.*] [Niranjan Chitrakar]

❄ Episode 3: Jaṭāyuvadha (the killing of Jaṭāyu)

Rāvaṇa is challenged by Jaṭāyu, a great bird warrior, son of Garuḍa and friend of Daśaratha, who confronts Rāvaṇa and grasps his chariot in his beak but lets it go for fear of injuring Sītā.[5]

Āraṇya.iii.1.

Jaṭāyu battles Rāvaṇa but is overcome. [Niranjan Chitrakar]

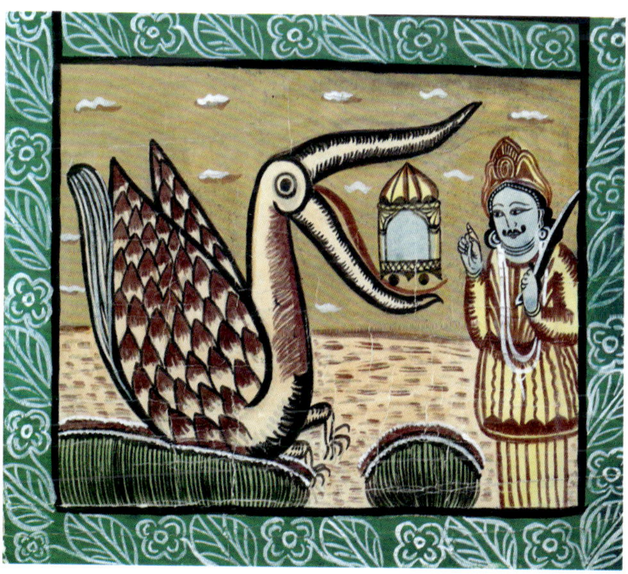

Āraṇya.iii.1.

5 Although in Kṛttivāsa's text it is Jaṭāyu's nephew Supārśva who tries to swallow Rāvaṇa's chariot, all paṭuās attribute the attempt to Jaṭāyu.

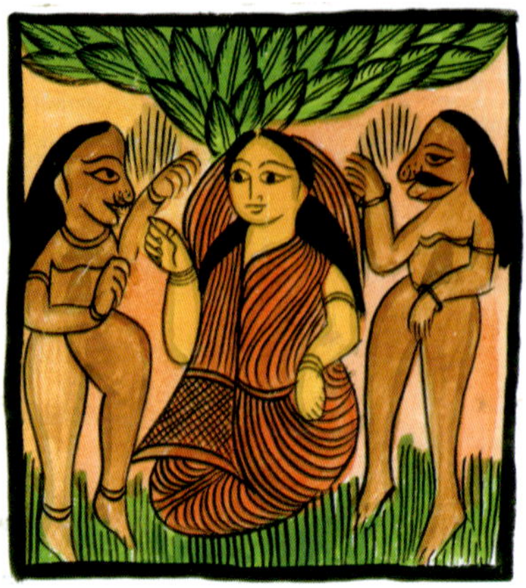

Āraṇya.iii.2 & 4.

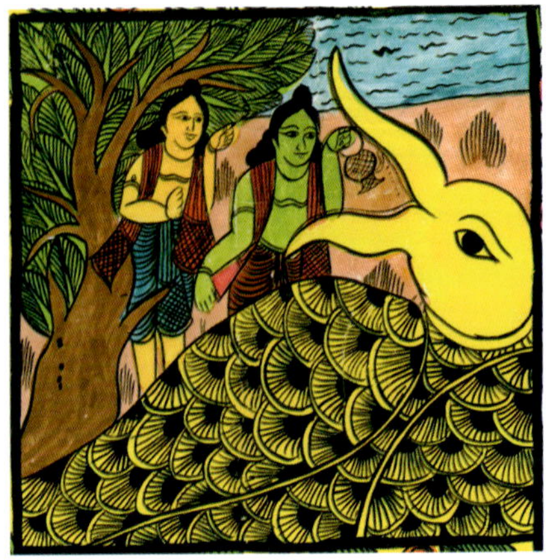

Āraṇya.iii.3.

Āraṇya.iii.2.

Rāvaṇa confines Sītā in his Aśoka grove, guarded by fierce cheḍīs (female ogres). [Khokan Chitrakar]

Āraṇya.iii.3.

Rāma and Lakṣmaṇa return to the hut to find it empty. As they wander about in search of Sītā, they come upon Jaṭāyu lying mortally wounded. He tells Rāma how he had tried to save Sītā from Rāvaṇa when Rāvaṇa was abducting her, but had failed to stop him. [Nurjahan and Khokan Chitrakar (mother and son)]

Āraṇya.iii.4.

Jaṭāyu also tells Rāma that Rāvaṇa is keeping Sītā confined in his Aśoka grove guarded by rākṣasīs. [Khokan Chitrakar][6]

---

6 In Kṛttivāsa's text, this information is given in the next part of the epic, the Kiṣkindhyākāṇḍa, by Jaṭāyu's elder brother Sampāti to the monkey army that travels south in search of Sītā. Paṭuās, however, bring this forward and attribute the revelation to Jaṭāyu.

Āraṇya.iii.5.

Jaṭāyu dies soon after [*and goes to heaven. Rāma performs funeral rites for him.*] [Khokan Chitrakar]

Āraṇya.iii.6.

Rāma is overcome with grief and lies down under a tree with Lakṣmaṇa consoling him. [Nurjahan and Khokan Chitrakar (mother and son)]

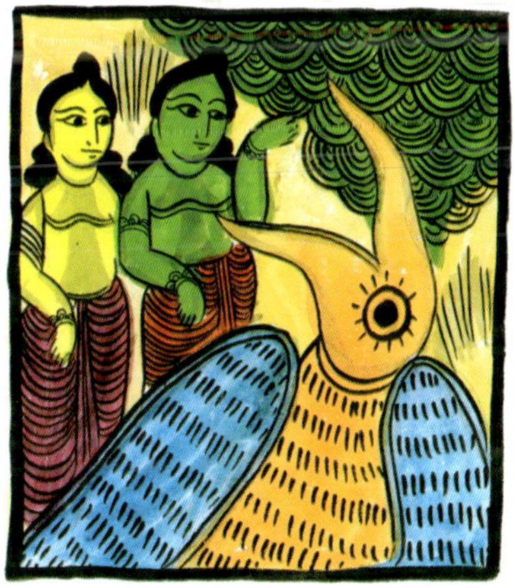

Āraṇya.iii.5.

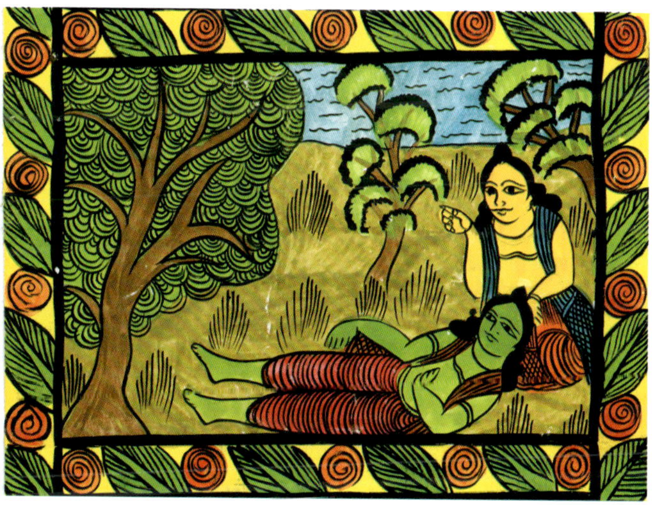

Āraṇya.iii.6.

[*Persuaded by Lakṣmaṇa, Rāma resumes the search, during which Rāma liberates Kabandha and Śabarī from their curses and they go to heaven; I have found no paṭa depicting these two events.*]

Here ends the third book, the Āraṇyakāṇḍa.

BOOK IV

KIṢKINDHYĀKĀṆḌA: ALLIANCE WITH MONKEYS AND THE SEARCH FOR SĪTĀ

Kiṣkindhyā is the forest kingdom of monkeys ruled by the mighty monkey king, Vāli. His younger brother Sugrīva has been driven out by Vāli for aspiring to the throne and is living in exile with a band of loyalists, including the great warrior Hanumān. While searching for Sītā, Rāma and Lakṣmaṇa meet them and they vow lifelong friendship. In return for Rāma's promise to kill Vāli and set Sugrīva on Kiṣkindhyā's throne, Sugrīva vows to help Rāma locate and rescue Sītā. Rāma kills Vāli unjustly from an ambush. Surprisingly, the paṭuās I know have not paid much attention to this important part of the epic, known as Vālivadha, memorialised in retellings of the *Rāmāyaṇa* in several genres, for instance in the kuṭiyāṭṭam dance-drama of Kerala. Only one frame in one of the paṭas I have shows this episode.

After Vāli's death, Sugrīva helps Rāma to search for Sītā by sending armies of monkeys east, west, north and south. The expedition to the south, about to give up the search, come upon a great wounded bird called Sampāti, Jaṭāyu's elder brother, who informs them that Rāvaṇa has taken Sīta to Laṅka across the ocean, where she is kept under vigilance in Rāvaṇa's Aśoka grove. Sampāti, who lost his wings while saving his younger brother Jaṭāyu from the scorching rays of the sun, regains his wings after listening to the *Rāmāyaṇa* recited by Hanumān. This encounter does not appear in the paṭas in my collection or in any others that I have seen.

❄ Episode 1: The alliance with Sugrīva

Rāma and Lakṣmaṇa meet a group of monkey warriors, who were driven out of their native land, and enters into an alliance with them.

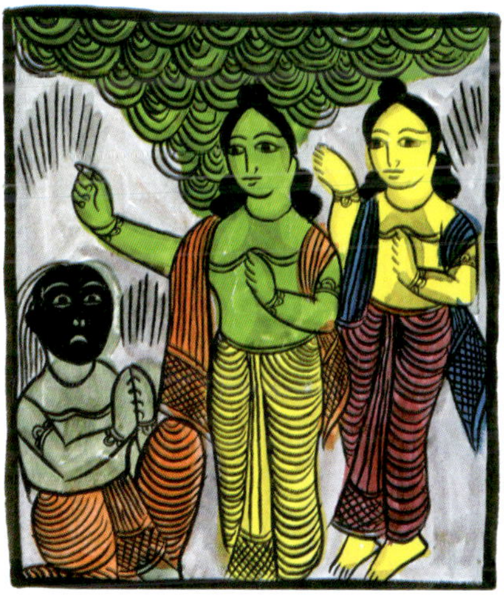

Kiṣkindhyā.i.1.

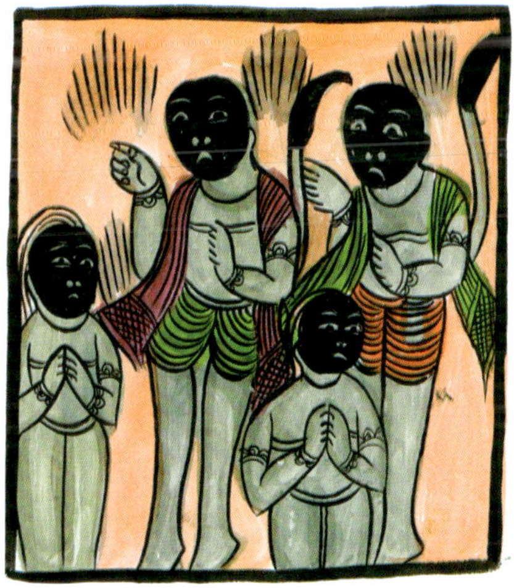

Kiṣkindhyā.i.2.

Kiṣkindhyā.i.1.

Rāma and Lakṣmaṇa meet a group of monkey warriors. [Khokan Chitrakar]

Kiṣkindhyā.i.2.

Sugrīva, the leader of the monkeys, and all his counselors declare their loyalty to Rāma [*and in return he promises to set Sugrīva on the throne of Kiṣkindhyā by killing the king, his brother Vāli*]. [Khokan Chitrakar]

❄ Episode 2: Vālivadha (the killing of Vāli)

Sugrīva challenges his brother to a duel. As they fight, Rāma kills Vāli from his hiding place. Sugrīva becomes king.

Kiṣkindhyā.ii.1.

Sugrīva and Vāli prepare to fight. [Khokan Chitrakar]

Kiṣkindhyā.ii.2.

Sugrīva becomes king of Kiṣkindhyā. [Khokan Chitrakar]

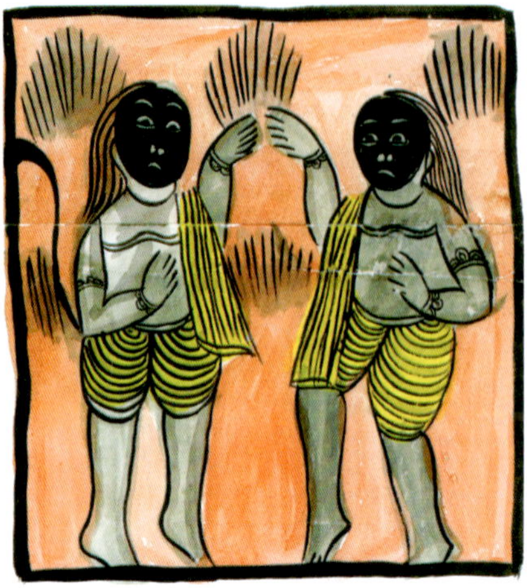

Kiṣkindhyā.ii.1.

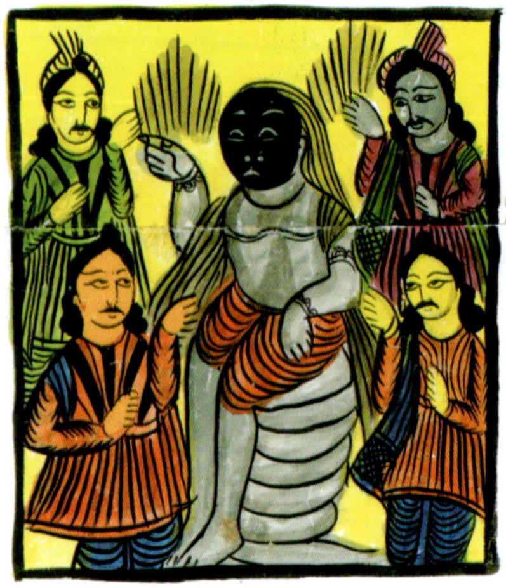

Kiṣkindhyā.ii.2.

Kiṣkindhyā.ii.3.
Sugrīva promises Rāma his services in finding Sītā. [Khokan Chitrakar]

[*The story goes on to describe the meeting of the monkeys with Sampāti who tells them that Sītā is living in captivity in Laṅkā, and their decision to cross the ocean to look for her. These episodes are left out of the paṭas in my collection. The information about Sītā's confinement in Laṅkā is mistakenly placed in the Āraṇyakāṇḍa and delivered by the dying Jaṭāyu, as noted earlier.*]

Here ends the fourth book, the Kiṣkindhyākāṇḍa.

BOOK V

SUNDARĀKĀṆḌA: THE MONKEYS SUCCEED IN THEIR SEARCH FOR SĪTĀ

To confirm Sampāti's information and to discover whether Sītā is indeed a captive in Laṅkā, Hanumān leaps across the ocean. He does find Sītā and in his jubilation, he defies Rāvaṇa and burns down much of Laṅkā before leaping back to his comrades. The monkeys return to Rāma to report their discovery and he leads them back to the shore of the ocean facing Laṅkā, preparing for an attack.

Meanwhile, in Laṅkā, Rāvaṇa's wise, virtuous brother Vibhīṣaṇa counsels him to surrender Sītā to Rāma, only to be kicked out—literally—from Rāvaṇa's presence. He seeks Rāma's favours and becomes his trusted counselor. They decide to build a bridge across the ocean, which is done by the monkey army, and they cross over to lay siege to Laṅkā.

❄ Episode 1: Rāma gains Vibhīṣaṇa's help

Vibhīṣaṇa arrives to join Rāma's camp after failing to persuade Rāvaṇa to return Sītā to Rama.

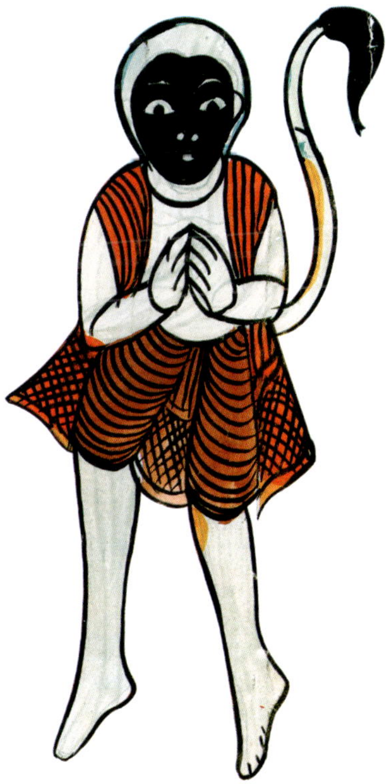

Sundarā.i.1.
The monkey army gathers by the ocean shore. [Nurjahan and Khokon Chitrakar]

Sundarā.i.2.
Vībhīṣaṇa arrives from Laṅkā to join Rāma. [Nurjahan and Khokon Chitrakar]

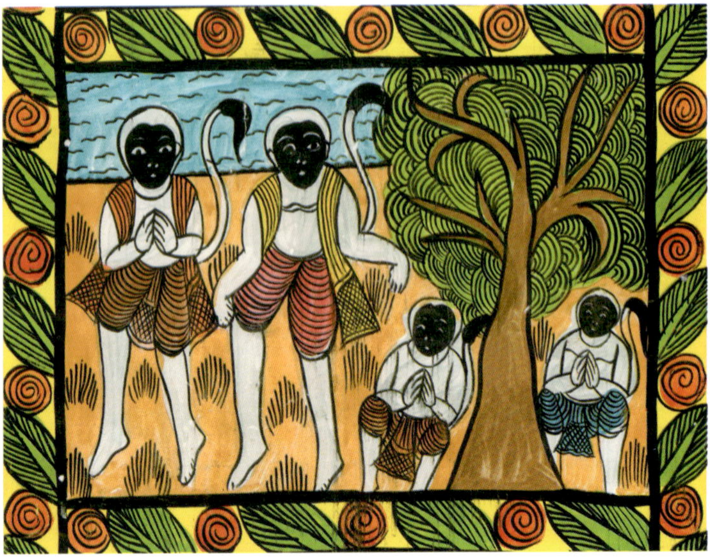

Sundarā.i.1.

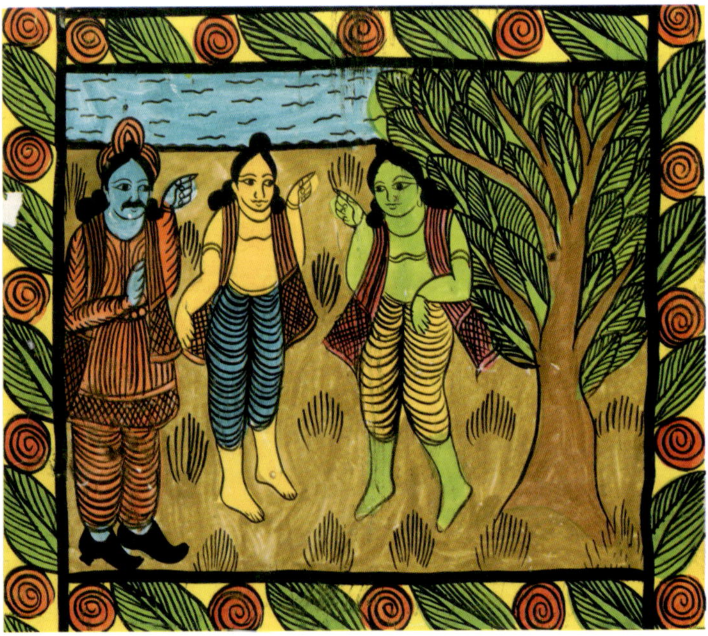

Sundarā.i.2.

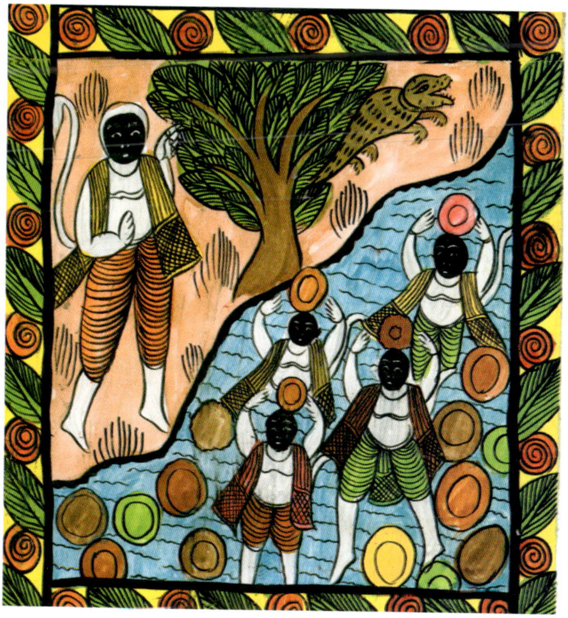

Sundarā.ii.1.

❄ Episode 2: Setubandhana (the bridge is built)

The monkeys build a bridge across the ocean and lay siege to Laṅkā.

Sundarā.ii.1 The monkeys carry rocks to the ocean to build the bridge to Laṅkā. [Nurjahan and Khokon Chitrakar]

Here ends the fifth book, the Sundarākāṇḍa.

BOOK VI

Laṅkākāṇḍa: The Battle at Laṅkā

This part of the epic is crowded with prodigious acts of valour on the part of all combatants. Rāma, Lakṣmaṇa and their monkey allies, such as Hanumān, Sugrīva and Aṅgad to mention only a few, are well matched by Rāvaṇa himself, his ogre-like brother Kumbhakarṇa, his commanders and his many sons, especially Indrajit, who is known as Meghanāda and can fight unseen from the sky. After a prolonged see-saw series of battles during which Rāma, Lakṣmaṇa and their entire army are almost vanquished, they secure the blessings of the gods, aided by whom and by employing some measure of trickery they put the rākṣasa army to rout. All rākṣasa heroes are killed, Rāvaṇa's entire clan is decimated, and finally Rāvaṇa himself is slain by Rāma. This climactic event is followed by a wholly unexpected one: after Sītā is freed from captivity and brought to Rāma, he declares that having lived under Rāvaṇa's power she may be deemed to have lost her honour and is no longer acceptable as his wife. Torn by his heartlessness, her public disgrace and outraged dignity, Sītā resolves to demonstrate her purity by putting herself to the ordeal of entering a burning pyre. When she does so, loudly lamented by Rāma himself and the assembled warriors, Lord Brahmā and other gods rush to reproach Rāma's rash suspicion, and Agnideva, the god of fire, leads her out of the flames and pronounces her unsullied chastity. The reunion of Rāma and Sītā is further blessed by the spirit of Daśaratha and they return to Ayodhyā, to the jubilation of all.

❄ Episode 1: Aṅgad visits Rāvaṇa's court

Carrying out Rāma's instructions, Vāli's son Aṅgad storms his way into Rāvaṇa's court to issue an insulting challenge and ultimatum to release

Sītā. This episode, known as "Aṅgader Rāibar" in Kṛttivā's version and many subsequent retellings of the incident in Bengali, actually comes later in this Book but is given precedence in my set of paṭas.

Laṅkā.i.1.

Aṅgad shows his defiance of Rāvaṇa by sitting on his coiled tail which places him higher than the enthroned rākṣasa king. [Nurjahan and Khokan Chitrakar]

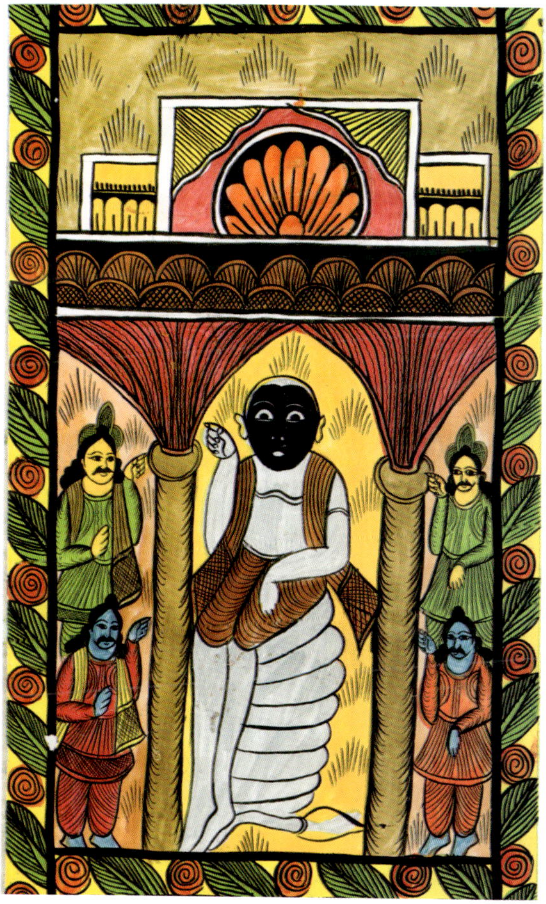

Laṅkā.i.1.

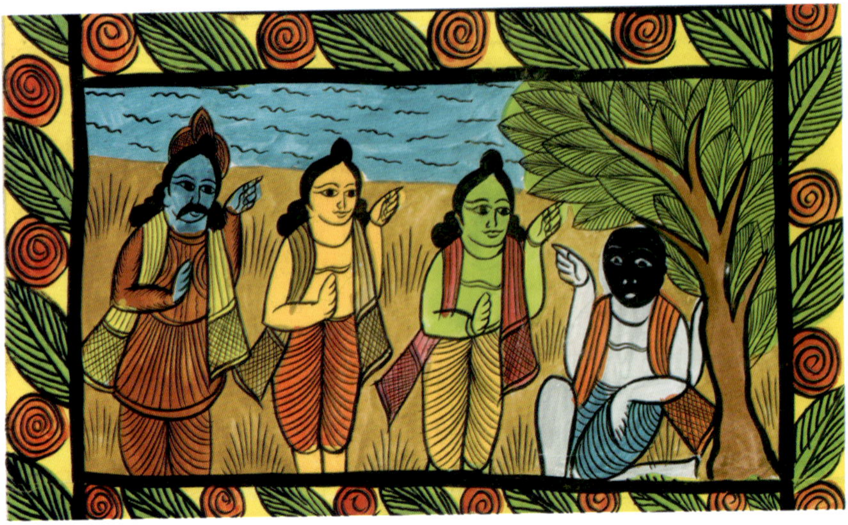

Laṅkā.i.2.

Laṅkā.i.2.

Aṅgad reports to Rāma, Lakṣmaṇa and Vibhīṣaṇa. [Nurjahan and Khokan Chitrakar]

❄ Episode 2: The battle begins

To assess Rāma's strength, Rāvaṇa mounts the city's fortifications. Rāma shoots at him and he flees. Later Rāma and Lakṣmaṇa have their first fight with Rāvaṇa.

Laṅkā.ii.1.

Rāma and Lakṣmaṇa look up to see Rāvaṇa up on the city wall and shoot arrows at him to send him fleeing. [Nurjahan and Khokan Chitrakar]

Laṅkā.ii.2.

Rāma and Lakṣmaṇa join battle with Rāvaṇa, with Hanumān watching. The result is inconclusive. [Khokan Chitrakar]

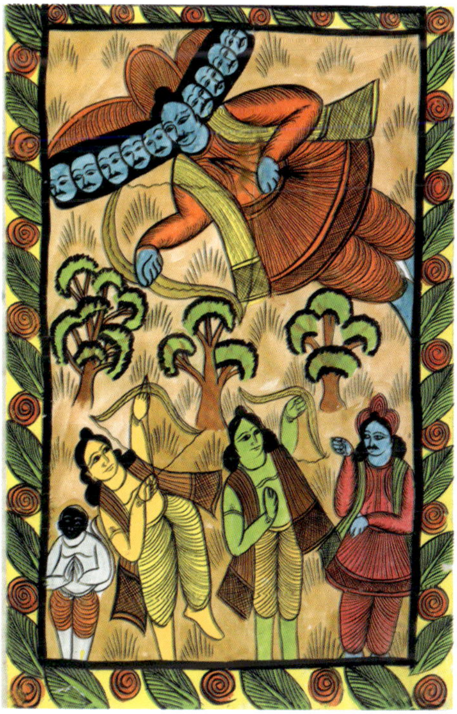

Laṅkā.ii.1.

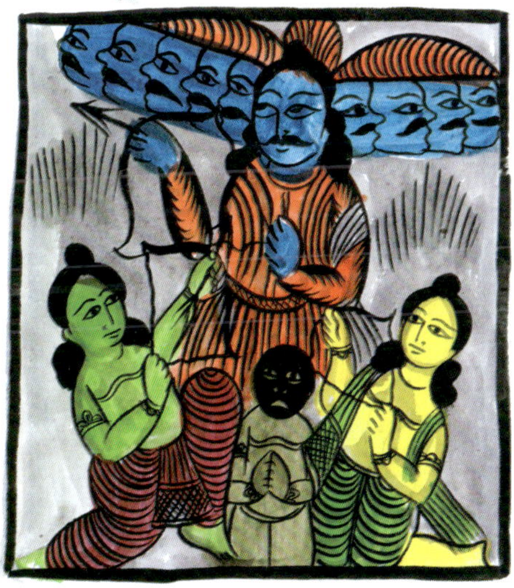

Laṅkā.ii.2.

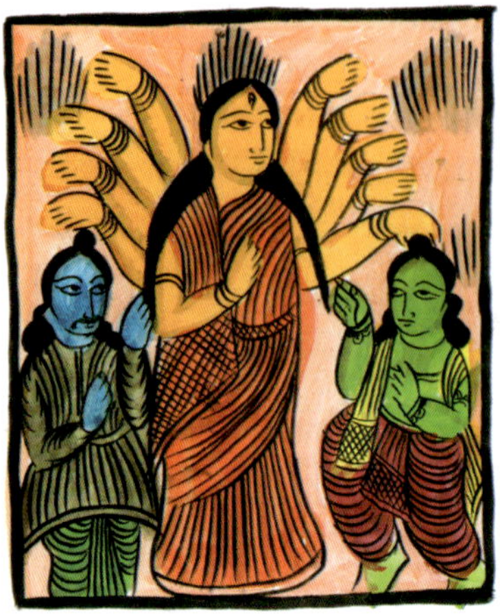

Laṅkā.iii.1.

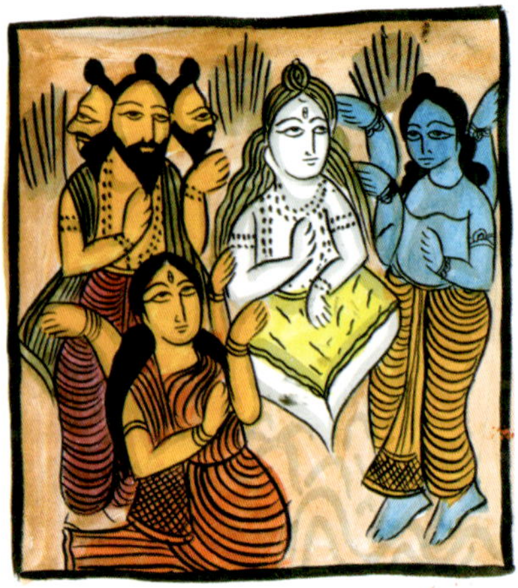

Laṅkā.iii.2.

❄ Episode 3: Rāma worships Durgā

Rāma calls upon the gods to come to his aid.

Laṅkā.iii.1.

Rāma worships Goddess Durgā. [Khokan Chitrakar]

Laṅkā.iii.2.

Brahmā, Śiva, Viṣṇu and a goddess (who may be Caṇḍikā, as suggested by her four arms; she makes a brief appearance in Kṛttivāsa (*KR*, p. 389) but not with the other deities) appears. This gathering of the deities is the painter's own invention. [Khokan Chitrakar]

Laṅkā.iii.3.

Rāma listens to Vibhīṣaṇa's advice (regarding the mode of worship). [Khokan Chitrakar]

Laṅkā.iii.4.

Rāma and Lakṣmaṇa instruct Hanumān to carry out a task. [Khokan Chitrakar]

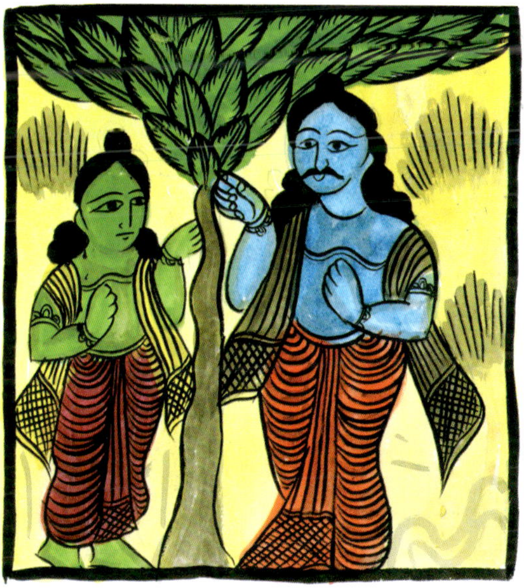

Laṅkā.iii.3.

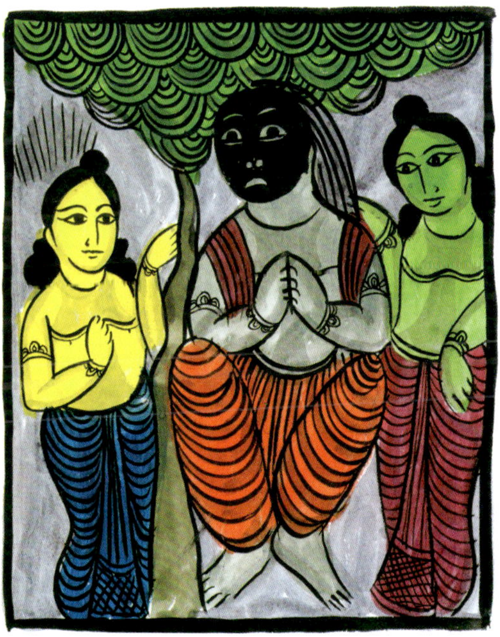

Laṅkā.iii.4.

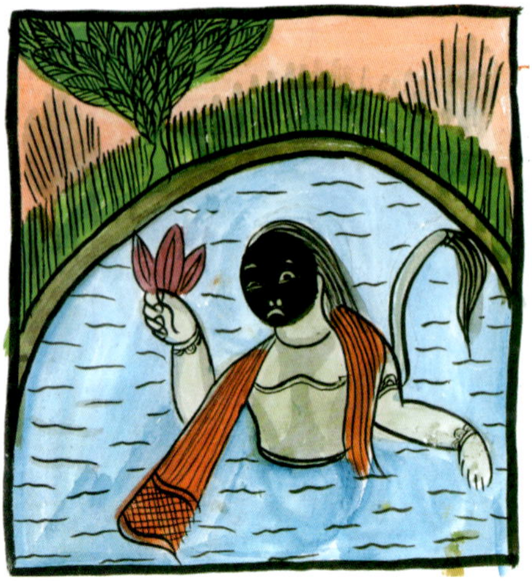

Laṅkā.iii.5.

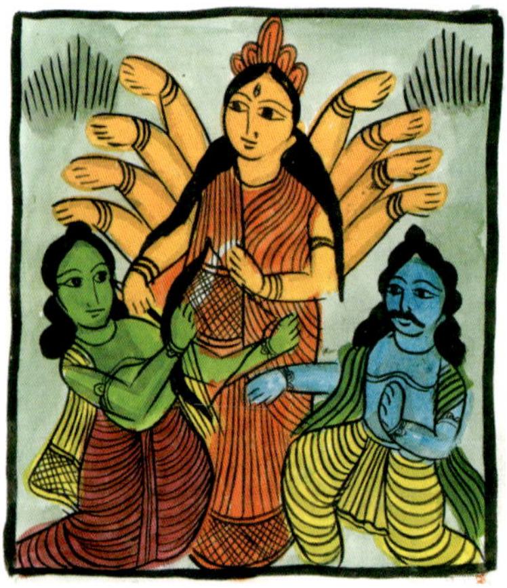

Laṅkā.iii.6.

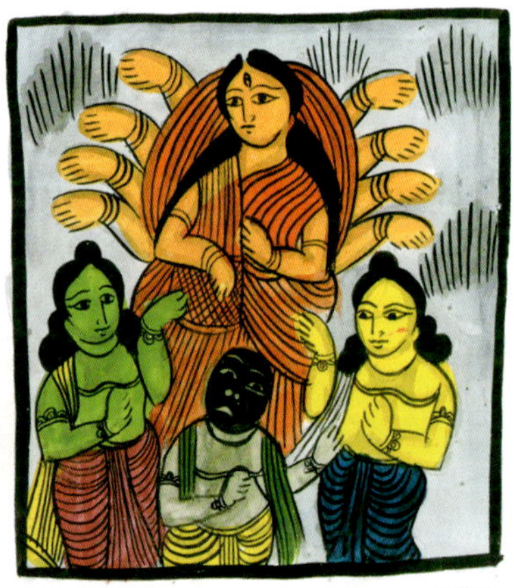

Laṅkā.iii.7.

Laṅkā.iii.5.
Hanumān plucks a lotus at Lake Devīdaha (a dark pink bloom here, although in Kṛttivāsa's account the lotus is blue). [Khokan Chitrakar]

Laṅkā.iii.6.
Rāma worships Durgā, watched by Vibhīṣaṇa. [Khokan Chitrakar]

Laṅkā.iii.7.
Rāma and Lakṣmaṇa worship Durgā, with Hanumān standing by. [Khokan Chitrakar]

❄ Episode 4: The killing of Mahīrāvaṇa:

Mahīrāvaṇa, son of Rāvaṇa, is the ruler of an underworld kingdom with supernatural powers gained by his devotion to Goddess Mahāmāyā. He kidnaps Rāma and Lakṣmaṇa and carries them down to his underworld city, where he intends to sacrifice them to the goddess. Hanumān follows them there and saves Rāma and Lakṣmaṇa by killing Mahīrāvaṇa.

Laṅkā.iv.1.
Hanumān finds Rāma and Lakṣmaṇa in Mahīrāvaṇa's temple. [Khokan Chitrakar]

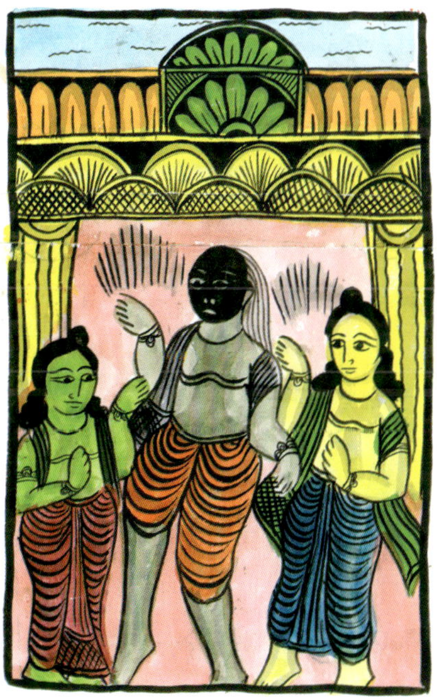

Laṅkā.iv.1.

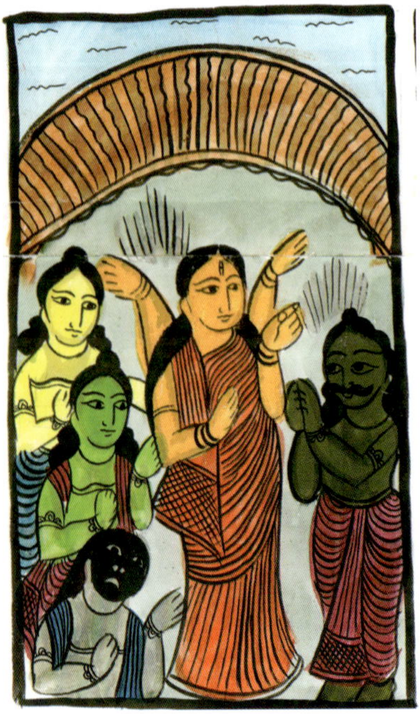

Laṅkā.iv.2.

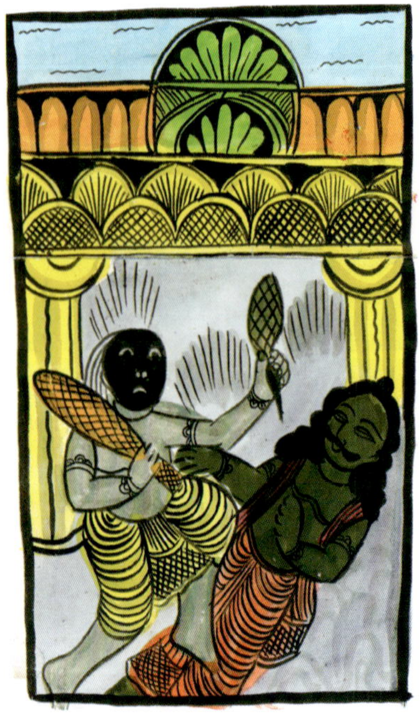

Laṅkā.iv.3.

Laṅkā.iv.2.
Mahīrāvaṇa brings Rāma and Lakṣmaṇa to the goddess, watched by Hanumān. [Khokan Chitrakar]

Laṅkā.iv.3.
Hanumān kills Mahīrāvaṇa. [Khokan Chitrakar]

❄ Episode 5: Stealing the magic arrow that carries the power to kill Rāvaṇa:

By Brahmā's decree, Rāvaṇa can be killed only by the arrow given to him by the god and since then kept hidden by Rāvaṇa's queen Mandodarī. When this secret is revealed to Rāma by Vibhīṣaṇa, Hanumān is commissioned to get the arrow from Mandodarī and he succeeds in doing so by trickery.

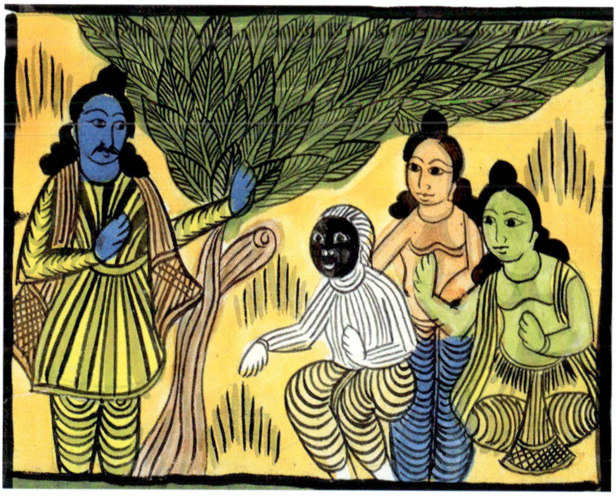

Laṅkā.v.1.

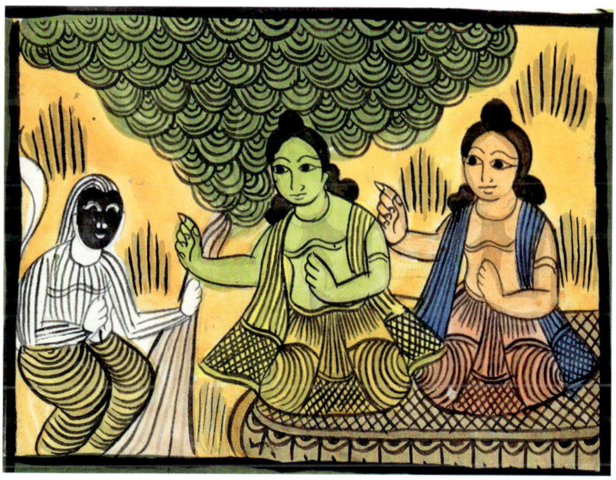

Laṅkā.v.2.

Laṅkā.v.1.

Vibhīṣaṇa tells Rāma and Lakṣmaṇa the secret of the arrow that Mandodarī keeps hidden. [Kalpana Chitrakar]

Laṅkā.v.2.

Rāma commands Hanumān to go and get the arrow. [Kalpana Chitrakar]

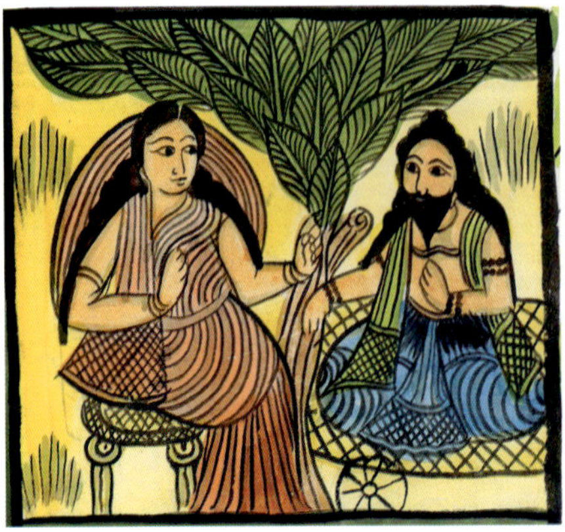

Laṅkā.v.3.

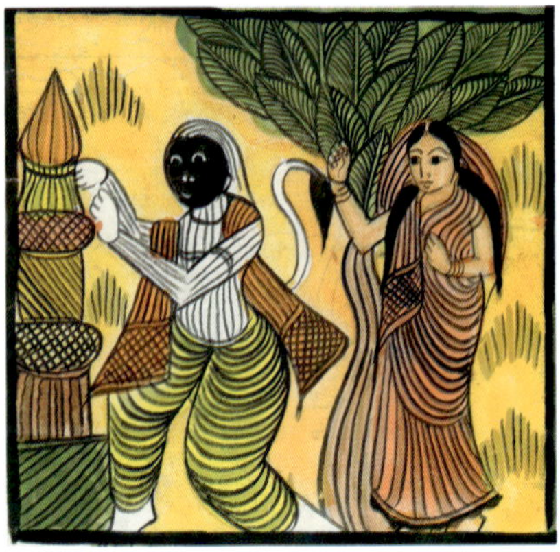

Laṅkā.v.4.

Laṅkā.v.3.
Hanumān goes to Mandodarī disguised as a holy man. [Kalpana Chitrakar]

Laṅkā.v.4.
Hanumān persuades Mandodarī to reveal where the arrow is hidden and steals it as Mandodarī watches in dismay. [Kalpana Chitrakar]

Laṅkā.v.5.
Hanumān brings back the arrow and presents it to Rāma, Lakṣmaṇa and Vibhīṣaṇa. [Kalpana Chitrakar]

Laṅkā.v.6.
Rāma approaches Rāvaṇa for their final battle, as Lakṣmaṇa, Vibhiṣaṇa and Hanumān watch. [Kalpana Chitrakar]

Laṅkā.v.7.
The final battle of Rāma and Rāvaṇa, with Hanumān, Lakṣmaṇa and Vibhīṣaṇa standing by. [Khokan Chitrakar]

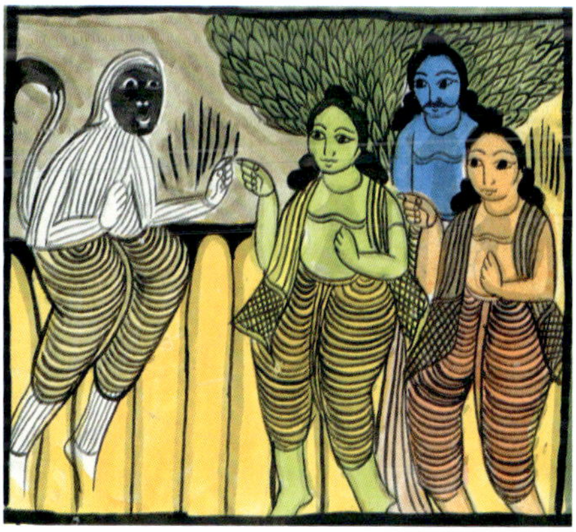

Laṅkā.v.5.

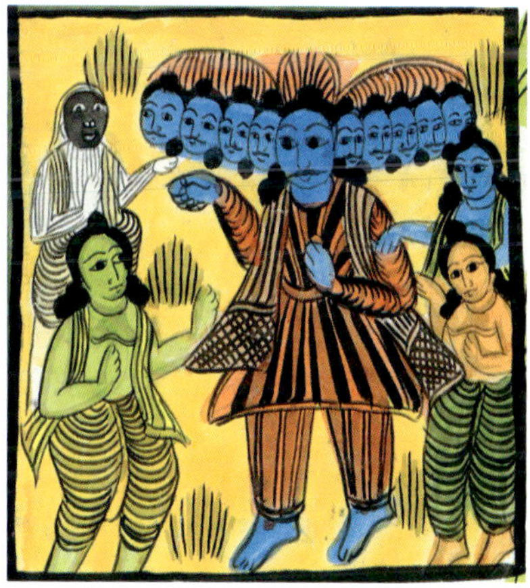

Laṅkā.v.6.

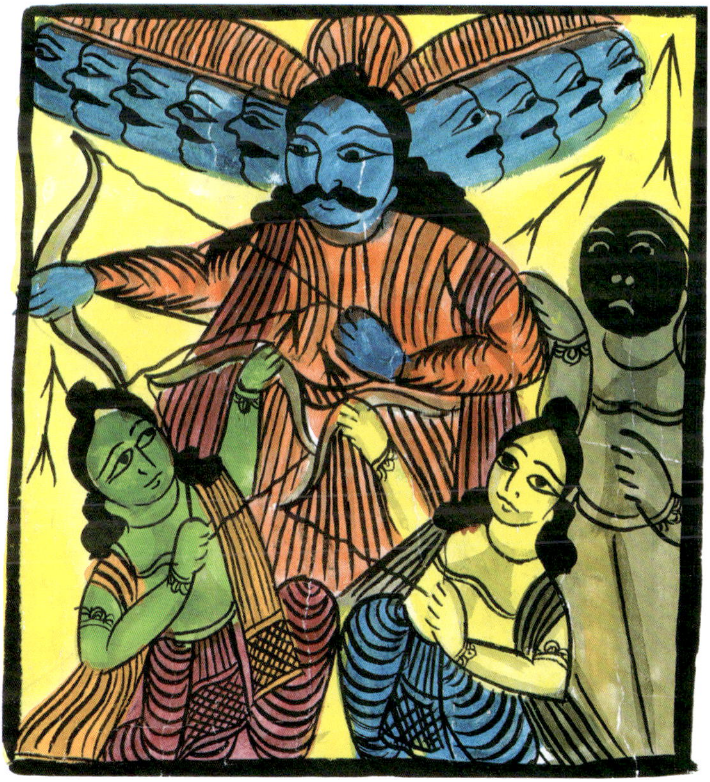

Laṅkā.v.7.

❄ Episode 6: The death of Rāvaṇa

Rāvaṇa's death brings an end to the battle.

Laṅkā.vi.1.

Rāvaṇa lies dead, mourned by his queens and Vibhīṣaṇa. [Khokan Chitrakar]

Laṅkā.vi.2.

Rāvaṇa on his funeral pyre. His regally adorned body has one head

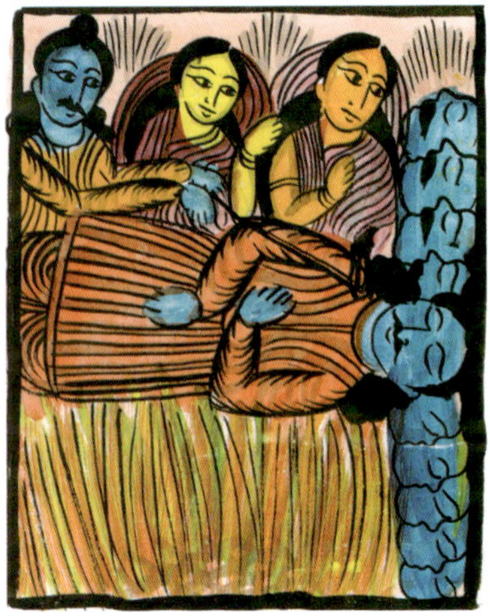

Laṅkā.vi.1.

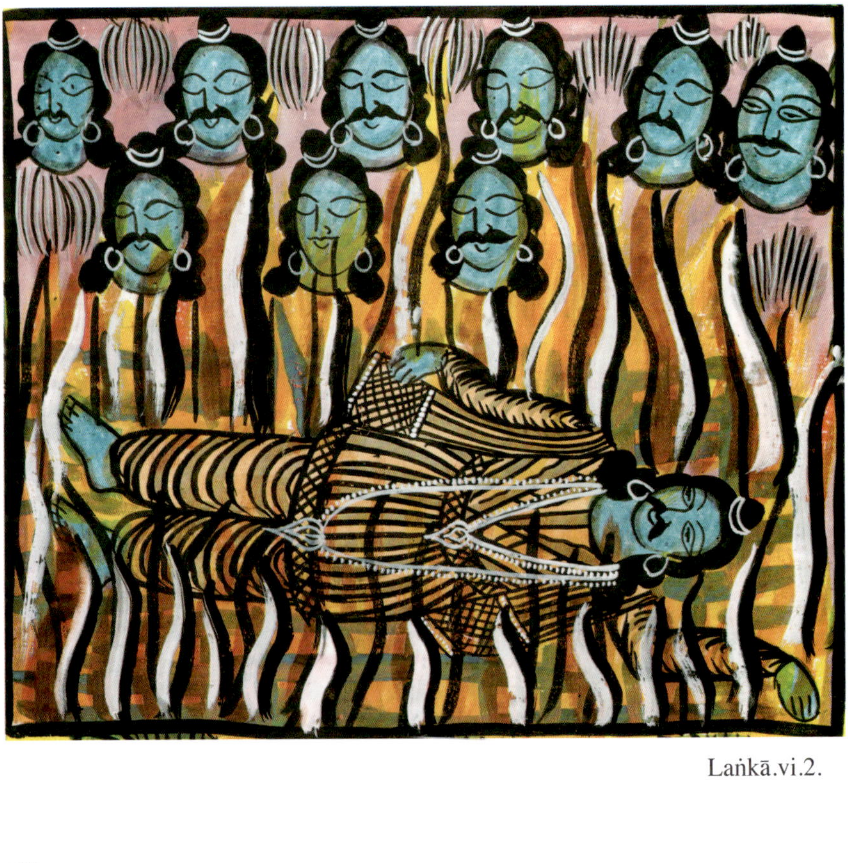

Laṅkā.vi.2.

attached to it while the other nine appear above the flames. [Niranjan Chitrakar]

❄ Episode 7: Sītā's agniparīkṣā ordeal by fire and the return of Rāma, Sītā and Lakṣmaṇa to Ayodhyā

Rāma refuses to take Sītā back because she might be suspected to have lost her honour as Rāvaṇa's captive. Deeply hurt and offended, she proves her purity by going through an ordeal by fire and her unsullied virtue is acclaimed by the assembled gods. Rāma and Sītā are reunited.

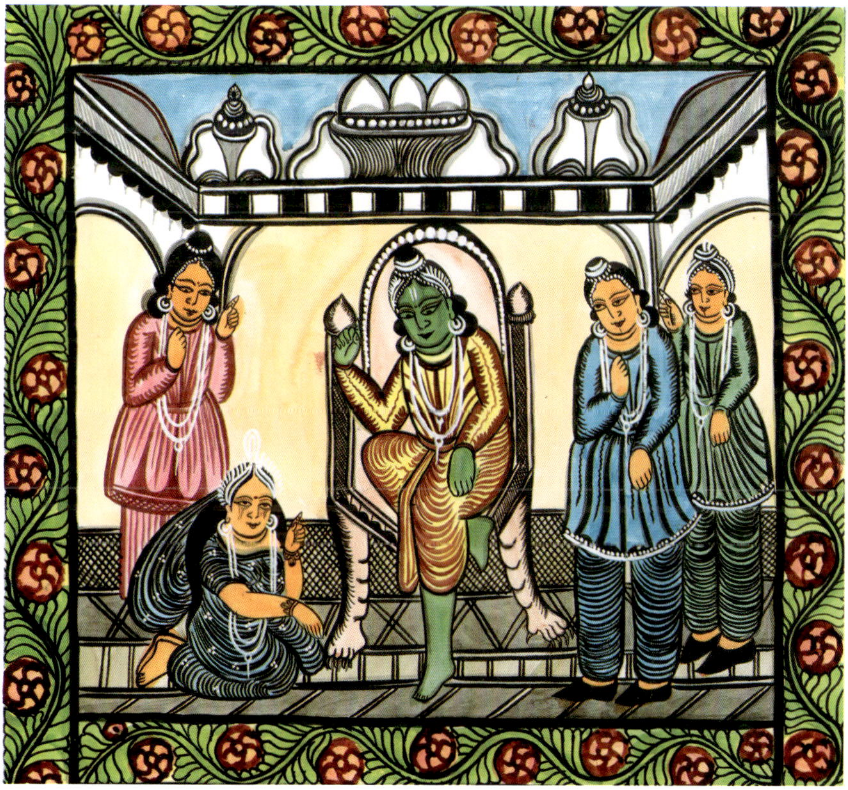

Laṅkā.vii.1.

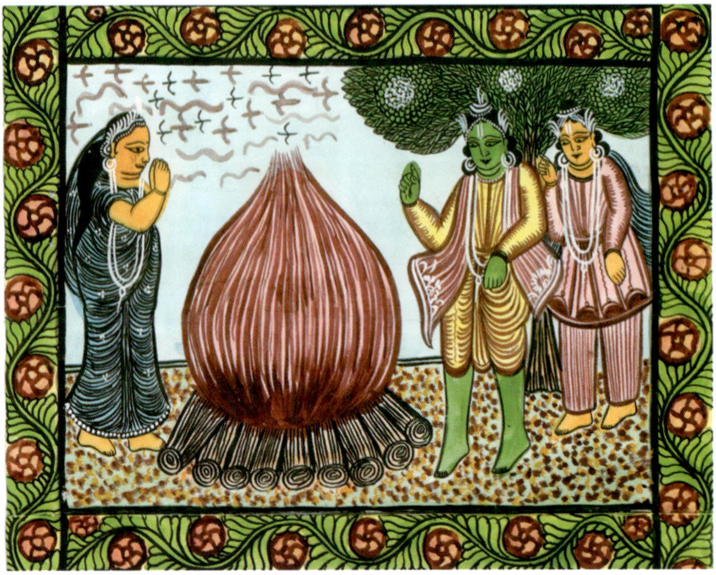

Laṅkā.vii.2.

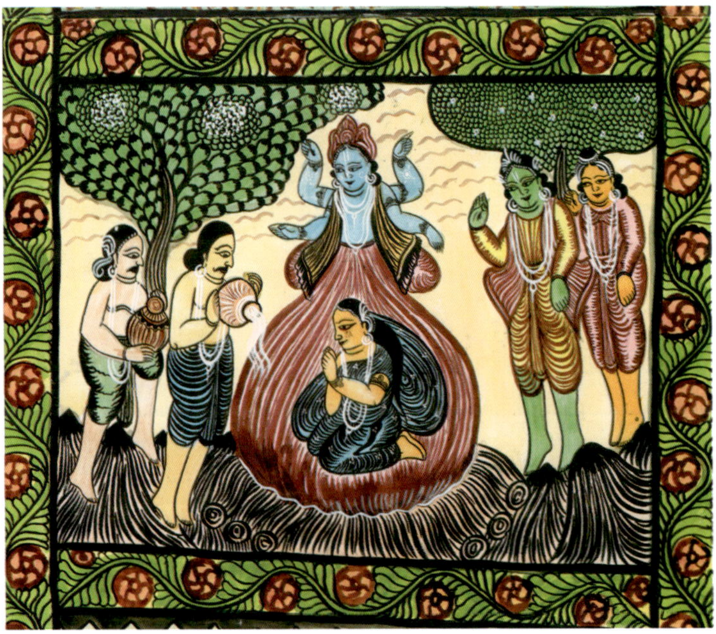

Laṅkā.vii.3.

Laṅkā.vii.1.

Brought to Rāma's presence after her rescue, Sītā bows down before Rāma, who is seated on a throne. [Niranjan Chitrakar]

Laṅkā.vii.2.

Sītā prepares to enter the burning pyre as Rāma and Lakṣmaṇa watch. [Niranjan Chitrakar]

Laṅkā.vii.3.

As Sītā sits within the pyre, the god of fire rises from the flames to pronounce her free of all blame. [Niranjan Chitrakar]

Laṅkā.vii.4.

Brahmā and Viṣṇu appear before Rāma. [Niranjan Chitrakar]

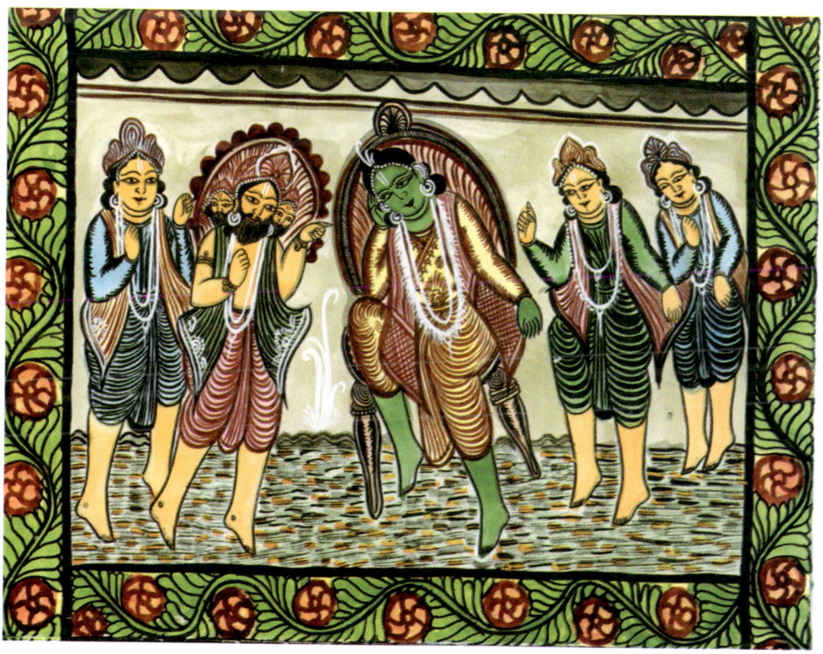

Laṅkā.vii.4.

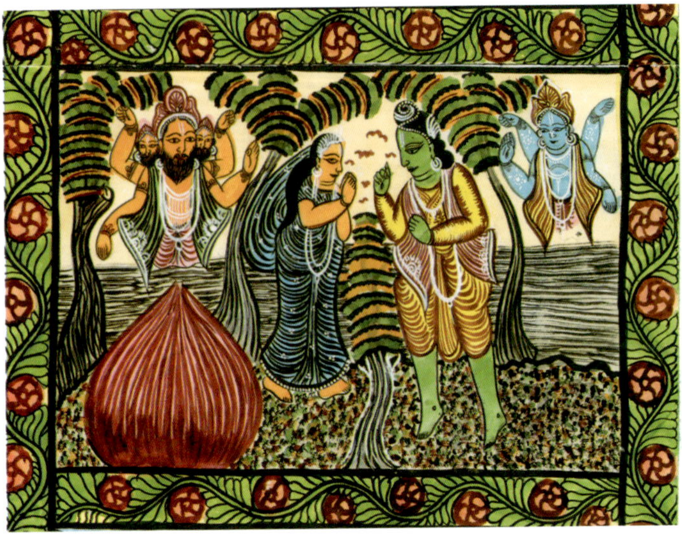

Laṅkā.vii.5.

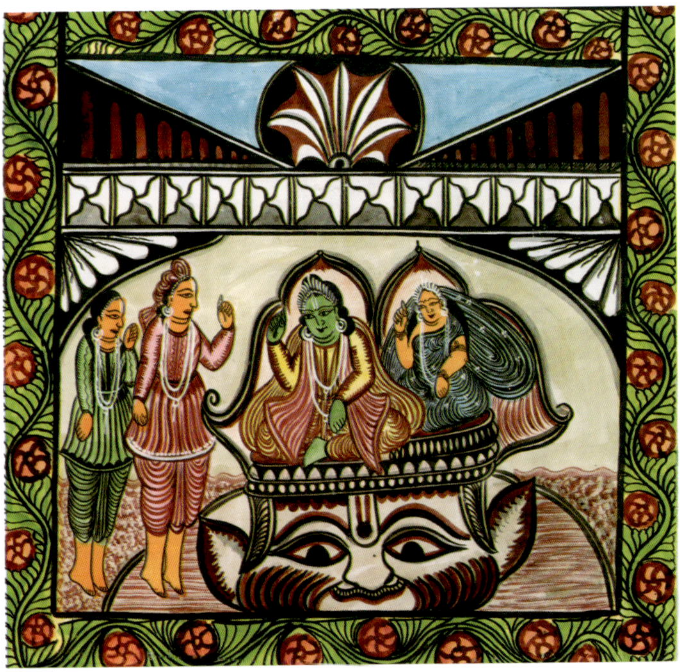

Laṅkā.vii.6.

Laṅkā.vii.5.

Rāma and Sītā are reunited in the presence of Brahmā and Viṣṇu. [Niranjan Chitrakar]

Laṅkā.vii.6.

Sitting on their throne, Rāma and Sītā are hailed as king and queen by Lakṣmaṇa and others. [Niranjan Chitrakar]

[*Rāma sets* Vibhīṣaṇa *on the throne of Laṅkā, rewards his monkey allies and returns to rule Ayodhyā with Sītā and Lakṣmaṇa*.]

Here ends Laṅkākāṇḍa, the sixth book of the *Rāmāyaṇa*.

BOOK VII

UTTARĀKĀṆḌA

After ruling Ayodhyā for many years, Rāma begins to hear reports of his subjects whispering their suspicion of Sītā's chastity after having been in Rāvaṇa's power, and wondering why Rāma allows her to be his queen. Rāma bows to public complaints despite having been assured of her pure character by Agnideva, the god of fire, when she put herself to an ordeal by fire after her rescue. He orders Lakṣmaṇa to conduct the pregnant Sītā to the forest and leave her there. But Vālmīki gives her shelter in his āśrama (hermitage) where her twin sons are born. They receive lessons from him in warfare and in the śāstras. They also learn to sing the *Rāmāyaṇa*.

Meanwhile, Rāma who is distraught at having had to exile Sītā, has been ruling Ayodhyā with her effigy (golden in most *Rāmāyaṇas* but not in these paṭa narratives). To assert his sovereignty, Rāma decides to hold the aśvamedha yajña, a ritual horse sacrifice that requires the sacrificial horse representing his authority to be led around the domain he claims to be the ruler of. His brother tours with the horse but when they reach Vālmīki's hermitage, Lava and Kuśa capture the horse and in the battle that ensues, they kill all of Rāma's forces and eventually Rāma himself, to be revived by Vālmīki. In some versions of the *Rāmāyaṇa*, as in the paṭas shown here, Rāma and his cohorts are made prisoner by the twins, to Sītā's outrage. Rāma returns to Ayodhyā without succeeding in learning the identity of the two boys.

Later, Vālmīki takes the twins to Rāma's court where they sing the *Rāmāyaṇa*, sending all listeners into transports of delight. Everyone, including Rāma, suspects they are his sons, and this is confirmed when they reveal they are Sītā's children. Repenting for having abandoned Sītā and been in the dark about his sons till now, Rāma calls for Sītā's return but still insists on putting her to yet another test of her virtue. Sītā is brought back and despite Vālmīki's forceful objections to putting her to the test, Rāma, who himself admits that he knows she is of unsullied virtue, still calls upon her to submit to a test.

Heartbroken that her humiliation seems never-ending, Sītā calls upon her mother, Prithivī, the Earth Goddess, to receive her for her final rest. The earth splits open and Prithivī rises in a golden throne to take Sītā in her arms and they descend into the earth even as Rāma tries to keep Sītā for himself by grasping her by her hair.

In the paṭas in my collection and in others I have seen, this is how the lives of Rāma and Sītā end.

❄ Episode 1: Scandal about Sītā

Rāma's subjects raise questions about Sītā's chastity after having been Rāvaṇa's captive.

Uttarā.i.1.

Rāma and Lakṣmaṇa recall Sītā's ordeal by fire. [Golap Chitrakar]

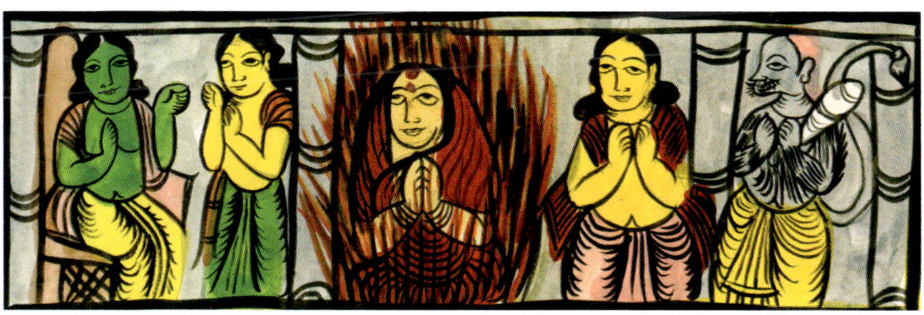

Uttarā.i.1.

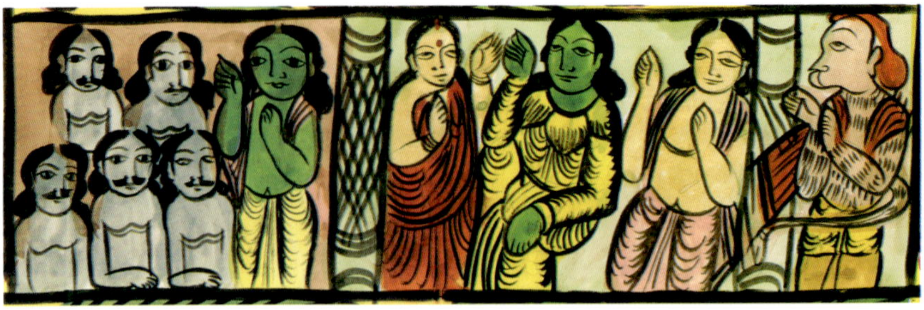

Uttarā.i.2.

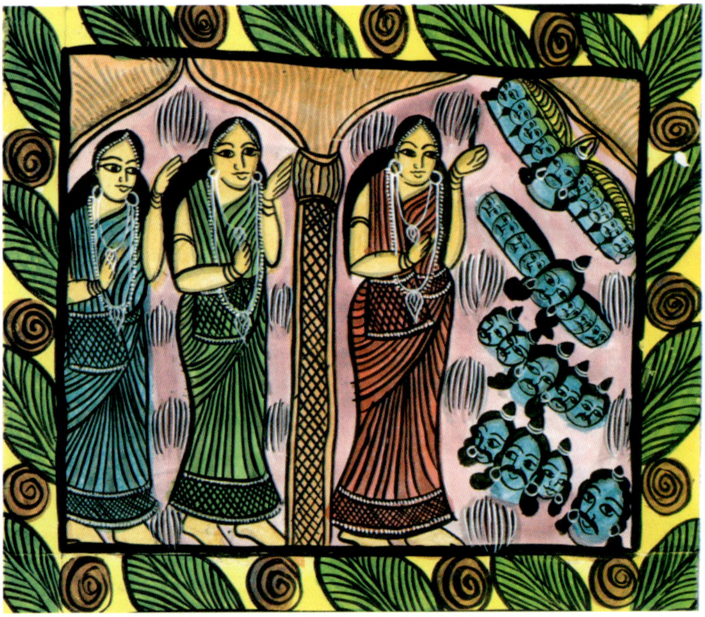

Uttarā.i.3.

Uttarā.i.2.

Rama listens to the complaints of his subjects and contemplates what is to be done with Sītā. [Golap Chitrakar]

Uttarā.i.3.

The women of the royal household persuade Sītā to draw a picture of Rāvaṇa. [Niranjan Chitrakar]

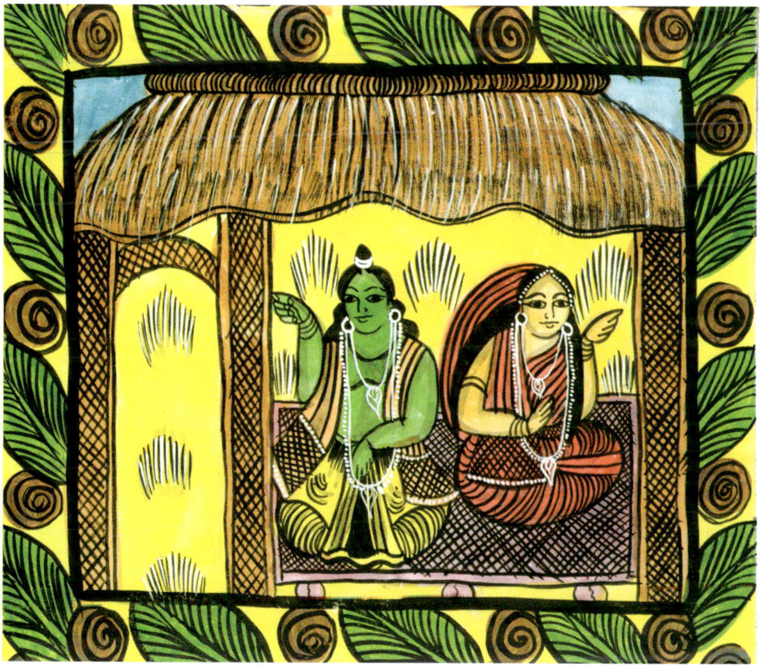

Uttarā.i.4.

Uttarā.i.4.
Rama turns away from Sītā. [Niranjan Chitrakar]

❄ Episode 2: Sītā's banabāsa (Sītā's exile)
Sītā is taken to the forest to be left there.

Uttarā.ii.1.
Lakṣmaṇa [*on Rāma's command*] invites Sītā to journey to the forest. [Niranjan Chitrakar]

Uttarā.ii.2.
Lakṣmaṇa conducts the pregnant Sītā to the forest in a chariot. [Golap Chitrakar]

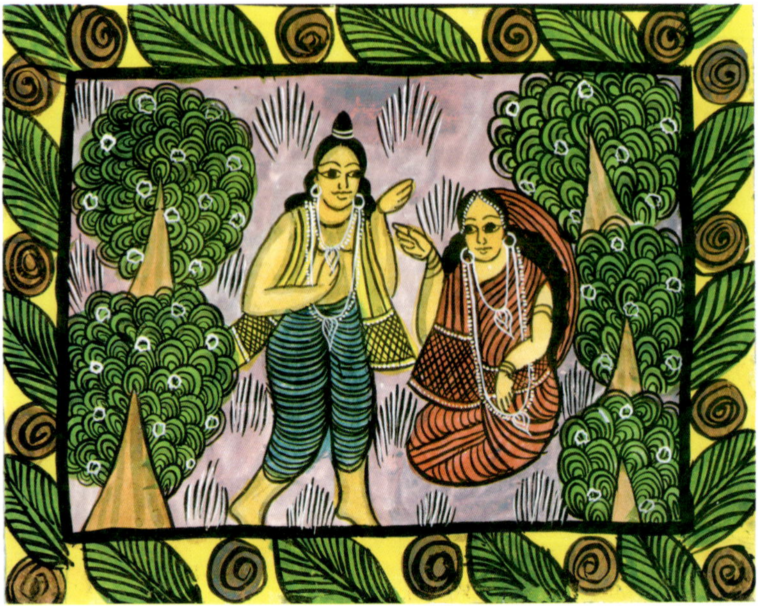

Uttarā.ii.1.

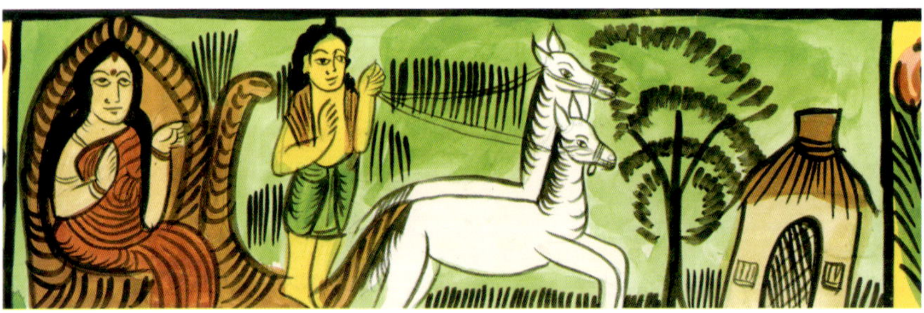

Uttarā.ii.2.

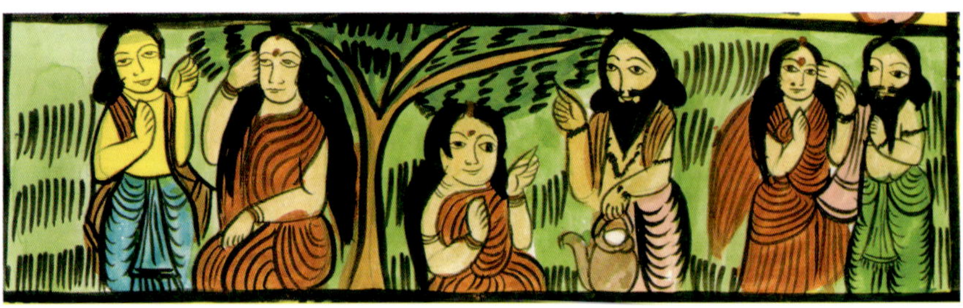

Uttarā.ii.3.

Uttarā.ii.3.

Lakṣmaṇa leaves Sītā at Vālmīki's hermitage where she is welcomed by the sage. [Golap Chitrakar]

❄ Episode 3: The birth of twin sons to Sītā

This story as told by the paṭuās I have met differs considerably from Kṛttivāsa's account or that of Vālmīki, where Sītā bears twin boys. In these paṭas, Sītā first gives birth to Lava. Soon after, she leaves him in Vālmīki's care to go to the river. Vālmīki somehow loses sight of Lava, and dismayed at having failed Sītā, he creates an exact replica of Lava out of a bundle of kuśa grass. Lava, however, is not really lost, so Sītā is overjoyed that she now has twin sons. This version of the birth of the twins comes from a widely dispersed folk tradition of the Rāma saga.

Uttarā.iii.1.

Sītā's son Lava is born at Vālmīki's hermitage. She takes him with her when she goes to the river. [Golap Chitrakar]

Uttarā.iii.2.

Not seeing the child at the hermitage, Vālmīki thinks he is lost and to comfort Sītā, he creates a replica of Lava out of kuśa grass. When Sītā returns with Lava, she is delighted that she now has a second son, twin

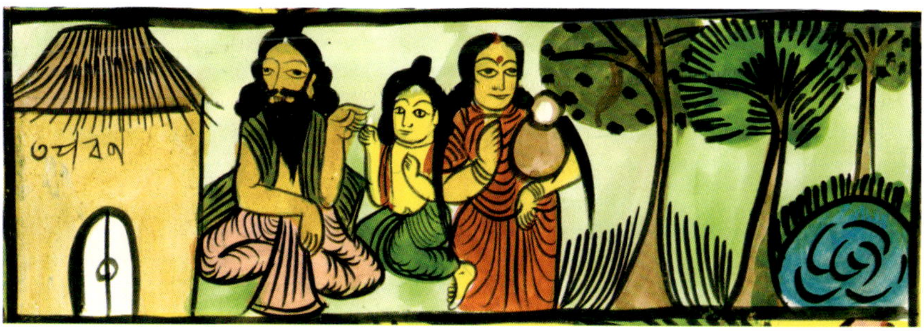

Uttarā.iii.1.

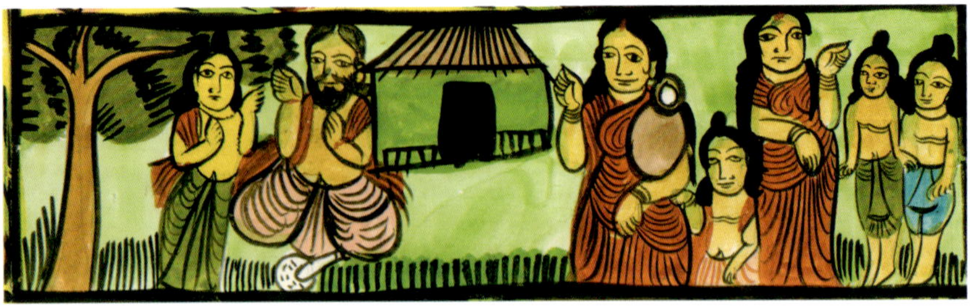

Uttarā.iii.2.

brother to Lava and thereafter the twins become inseparable. [Golap Chitrakar]

❄ Episode 4: Lava and Kuśa battle Rāma's armies to capture his sacrificial horse

The twins exhibit their prowess, which leads the way to recognising their parentage.

Uttarā.iv.1.

Rāma's sacrificial horse is captured by Lava and Kuśa. [Golap Chitrakar]

Uttarā.iv.2.

In the battle that ensues, the twins defeat Rāma's brothers and then Rāma himself, taking them prisoners. When they bring them to show their mother, she is shocked by their impudence. [Golap Chitrakar]

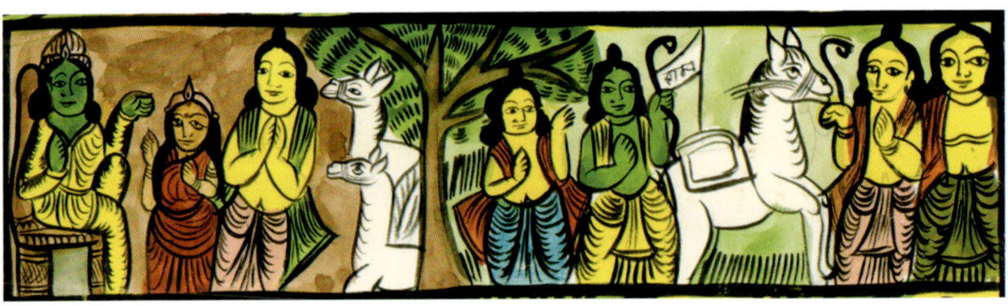

Uttarā.iv.1.

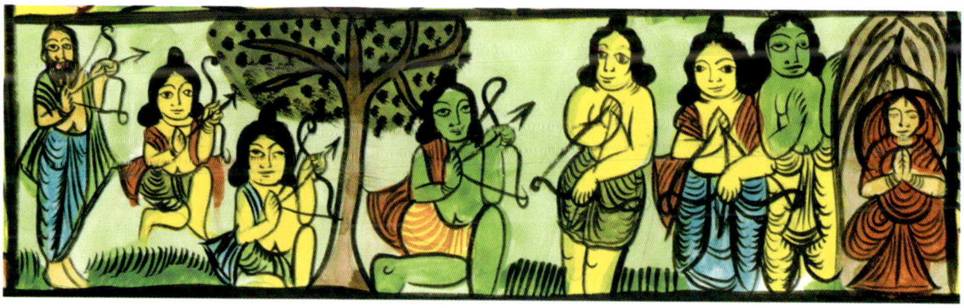

Uttarā.iv.2.

❄ Episode 5: Lava and Kuśa are recognised as Rāma's sons

The appearance of the twins leads to the happy event of their recognition as Rāma's sons but also lays the ground for Rāma to summon Sītā only to put her to a test of her virtue.

Uttarā.v.1.

Vālmīki takes Lava and Kuśa to sing the *Rāmāyaṇa* at Rāma's court in Ayodhyā. [Niranjan Chitrakar]

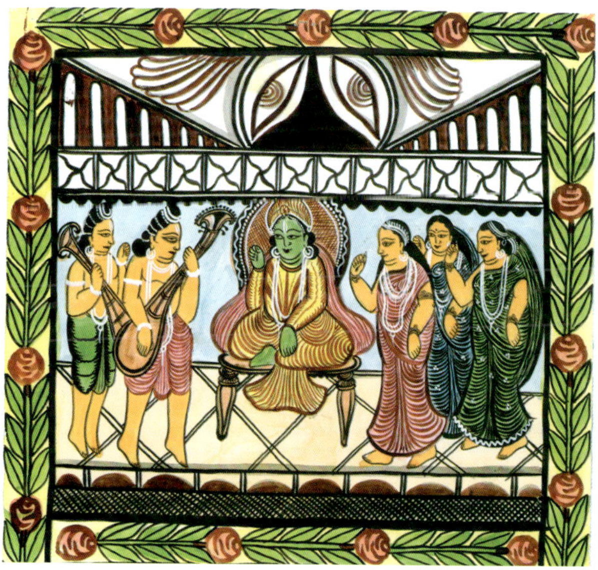

Uttarā.v.1.

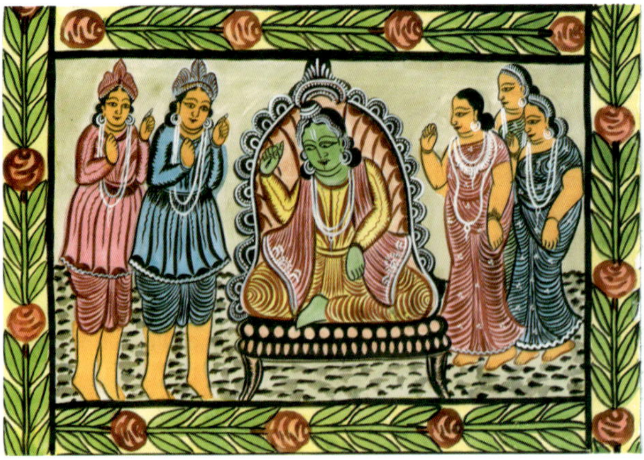

Uttarā.v.2.

Uttarā.v.2.

Father and sons are reunited, to the joy of three palace women (very likely the queen mothers, Kauśalyā, Kaikeyī and Sumitrā). [Niranjan Chitrakar]

❄ Episode 6: Sītā's final ordeal

Sītā arrives at Rāma's court and bewails her misfortune at having to prove her virtue repeatedly. Compelled by Rāma to do so again, she prays to her mother Prithivī, the Earth Goddess, to let her rest in peace. The earth splits open and Sītā sinks into the rift as Rāma tries to hold her back by grasping her by her hair.

Uttarā.vi.1.

Rama admits to Viṣṇu, Śiva and Brahmā that he knows Sītā is innocent of all blemish. [*This does not appear in Kṛttivās's Rāmāyaṇa*] [Niranjan Chitrakar]

Uttarā.vi.2.

Sītā bows to Rāma as the earth shows signs of breaches in its surface, watched by Kṛṣṇa and a woman (possibly one of the senior queens). [Niranjan Chitrakar]

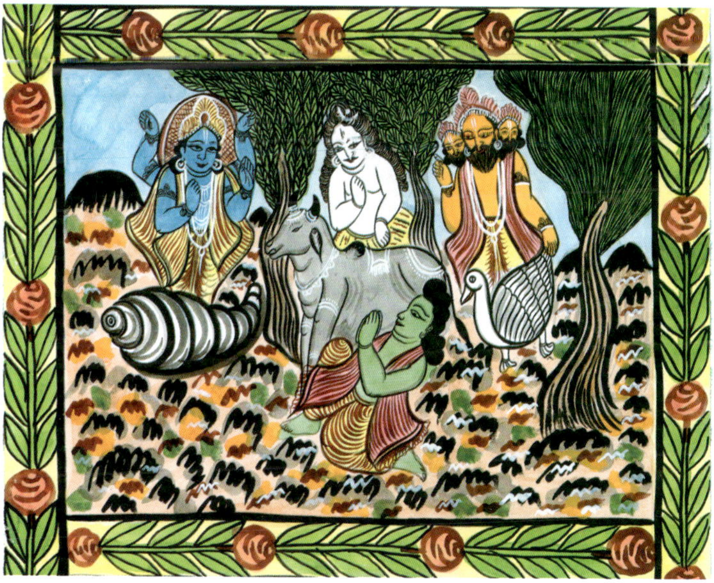

Uttarā.vi.1.

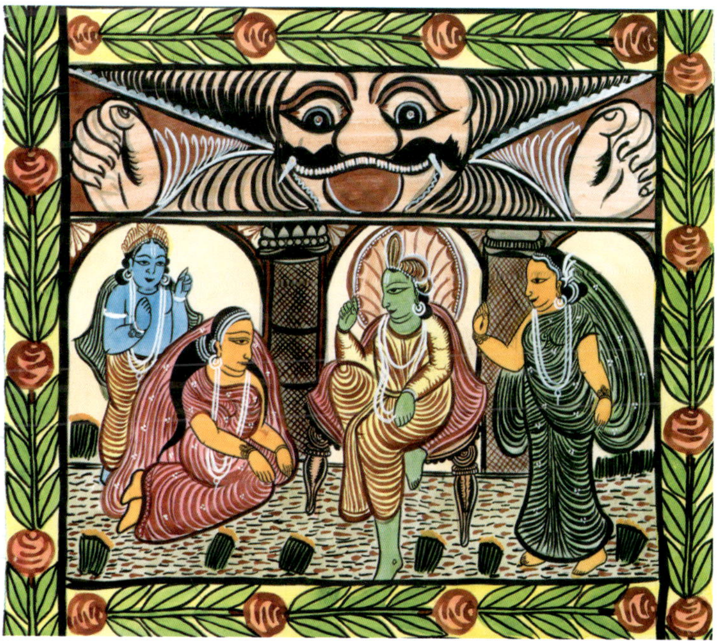

Uttarā.vi.2.

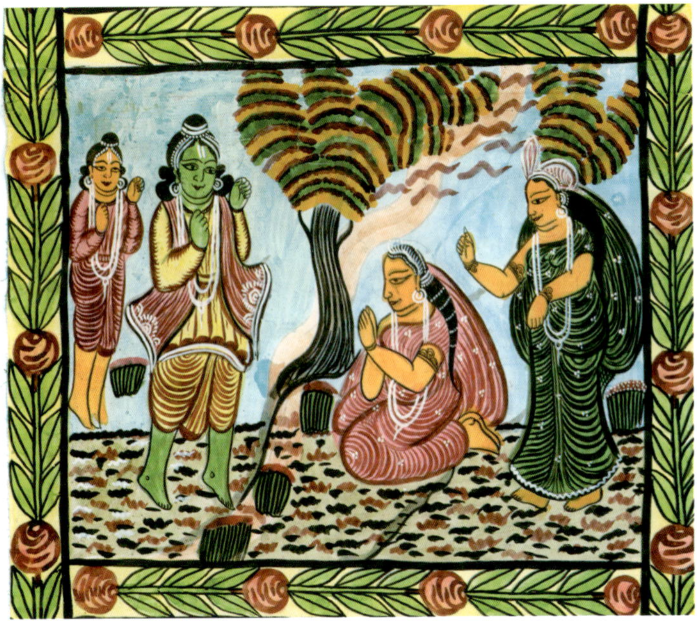

Uttarā.vi.3.

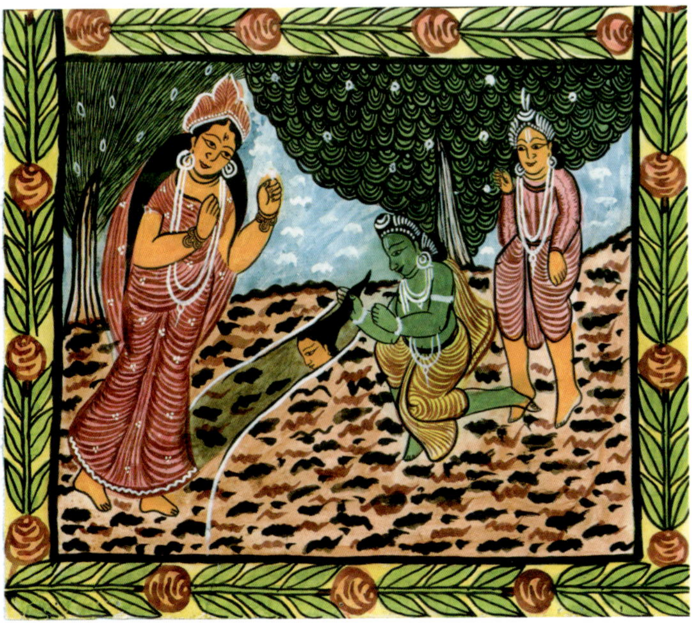

Uttarā.vi.4.

Uttarā.vi.3.

Sītā kneels before the breaches in the earth, praying to her mother the Earth Goddess, as Rāma, one of their sons and a queen look on. [Niranjan Chitrakar]

Uttarā.vi.4.

Sītā sinks into the earth, disappearing forever despite Rāma's attempt to hold her back by her hair. [Niranjan Chitrakar]

Here ends the *Rāmāyaṇa* as narrated in the Bengali paṭacitras from Medinipur.

summing up

The art of the paṭuās is derived from long-established traditions of storytelling, artistic form, technique and—where received narratives are concerned—ethical judgments. In the paṭas we see a community art that expresses a distinct community's ways of thinking, that of the paṭuās, about past and present, representing human experience through inherited conventions refracted by the light of the world around them. This is not an art that rests on adventurous leaps of the individual imagination but on shared views, narratives and performance strategies. Especially where subjects and themes have been handed down through generations and reiterated in line, colour and recitative voice, paṭuās choose to stay within the sets of experience common to their families or indeed to their wider community of performative practice. It is not that individuals lack originality; in the images reproduced on the preceding pages, distinctions are obvious in matters of the use of colours, lines and motifs, for instance in the design of borders, in the forms, postures and gestures of the figures peopling the paṭas, or in the forms of vegetation. The technique of the painters is firmly determined both by their inherited conventions as well as by the media they use, such as paint—bright primary colours being favourites—and paper or fabric. In addition, there is, of course, always, the matter of differences in skill. The difference in choosing the narrative material may seem muted as the pool of narrative nodes is commonly shared, as is the general structure of the storyline despite occasional variations. Again, this is clearly in evidence in the set of paṭas presented here, for the general plot of the *Rāmāyaṇa* was fixed centuries ago, and although individual artists insert or withhold bits and pieces of action, as noted in the comments on individual paṭas and episodes, they do cling to the main line of the Rāma saga.

It needs to be emphasised that the general trend of following the established story does not prevent departures from the standard story or the incursion of local variations. And that is one of the reasons why the *Rāmāyaṇa* of the Bengali paṭas is so worth studying. Consider the narrative variations. Why, for instance, is the Ayodhyākāṇḍa left out of all the *Rāmāyaṇa* paṭas? Why blank out the deadly scheming of Mantharā and Kaikeyī? One would think that reinforcing sympathy for Rāma and extolling his exemplary filial self-sacrifice to keep his father's vow would be just the right kind of celebration of Rāma the Righteous. Can that be the reason for withholding the depiction of Rāma's treacherous killing of Vāli from ambush? Silence over this dishonorable act may explain why the slaying of Indrajit, when he is vulnerable at worship, is similarly left untouched. But this speculation raises an even more troubling question: if the intent is to gloss over events of discredit to Rāma, then why highlight his inexplicable and repeated humiliation of Sītā?

The story that the paṭas tell is fascinating precisely because of these departures from the standard *Rāmāyaṇa* plot, including Kṛttivāsa's, the version that the paṭuās follow in the main and which already contains material outside Vālmīki's tale. As the narrative pieced together here from the work of a range of painters shows, we have a distinctly different *Rāmāyaṇa* in their oeuvre. It is the classic story no doubt, but one that draws upon the folk narrative tradition of eastern *Rāmāyaṇas*, whose distinctive nature has been firmly outlined by William Smith (1988), a tradition that confirms eastern India's cultural relationship with Southeast Asia.

But it is not only narrative innovations that distinguish the Bengali *Rāmāyaṇa* paṭas. It is also the implicit emotional engagement of the paṭuās with their subject, especially Sītā and her unceasing suffering, that creates a common ethical climate of empathy with the disempowered of the world. This is perhaps more clearly articulated in the lyrics the paṭuās sing in accompaniment to the images they unfold. That performance mode takes the still pictures out of the fixed complex of line and colour into the realm of an evolving performance and humanises icons into that of the fluid art of theatre. The show-and-tell mode is therefore a vital part of the totality of the art of the paṭuās and links it to the historical antecedents of the performing arts of India; we have seen this in the display of yamapaṭas in the *Harṣacarita*. The aesthetic of viewing frames of action, separate as they are, is complemented by the voiced commentary, creating an emotional and ethical totality of communication, empathic yet distanced from the viewer.

I do not claim this as an artistic project unmatched anywhere else. But the Bengali *Rāmāyaṇa* paṭas are indeed distinctive in that taken together they represent a commonality of form and substance, a remarkable cultural achievement precisely because it is the product of so many hands and minds working together. It is in this coming together of a community of imagination that the Bengali *Rāmāyaṇa* paṭas have created a niche for themselves.

references

Bāṇabhaṭṭa. 1985. *Harṣacaritam*. With explanatory notes by Shri Mohanadevapant. Delhi: Motilal Banarsidass.

Bandyopadhyaya, Debashish. 1972. *Bīrbhūmer Yamapaṭa o Paṭuā*. Calcutta: Subarnarekha.

Bhāsa. 1951. *Svapnavāsavadattam*. Edited by. P. P. Sharma. Allahabad: Rāma Narain Lal Publishers and Booksellers.

Bose, Mandakranta, ed. 2003. *The Rāmāyaṇa Culture: Text, Performance and Iconography*. New Delhi: D. K. Printworld. Second revised edition of *A Varied Optic: Contemporary Studies in the Rāmāyaṇa*. Vancouver: Institute of Asian Research at the University of British Columbia, 2000.

Bose, Mandakranta, ed. 2004. *Rāmāyaṇa Revisited*. New York: Oxford University Press.

Bose, Mandakranta and Sarika Priyadarshini Bose. 2010. *A Woman's Rāmāyaṇa: Candrāvati's Bengali Epic*. London: Routledge.

Bose, Mandakranta. 2010. "Sanskrit Ramayanas, Puranas and Rāma *Kavyas*: A Study in Evolution and Impact." In Krishnan 2010: 18–27.

Bose, Mandakranta. 2015. "The Killing of Sindhu in the Painted Scrolls of Bengal." In Kaushal, Bhalla and Pant 2015: 234–240.

Chattopadhyaya, Jyotsna. 2008. *Rāmāyaṇer Aitihya: Deśe Videśe*. Calcutta: Parul Prakashani.

Coomaraswamy, Ananda K. 1985 [1926]. *History of Indian and Indonesian Art*. New York: Dover Publications.

Dallapiccola, Anna L., ed. 2011. *Indian Painting: The Lesser-known Traditions*. New Delhi: Niyogi Books.

Forbes, Geraldine, and Lisa Langlois. 2010. "Patas and the Makers: Visual Culture in West Bengal." Picture Scrolls from India Exhibition catalogue. Oswego: Tyler Art Gallery, State University of New York at Oswego.

Ghose, Benoy. 1981. *Traditional Arts and Crafts of West Bengal: A Sociological Survey*. Calcutta: Papyrus.

Gurusaday Museum. 2008. *Album of Art Treasure: Scroll Painting*. Kolkata: Gurusaday Dutt Folk Art Society.

Jain, Jyotindra. 1999. *Kalighat Painting: Images from a Changing World*. Ahmedabad: Mapin Publishing.

Jefferson, Pilar. 2014. "The Art of Survival: Bengali Pats, Patuas and the Evolution of Folk Art in India." *Independent Study Project* (ISP) Collection. Paper 1815, pp. 41. http://digitalcollections.sit.edu/isp_collection/1815

Kālidāsa. 1994 [1968]. *Abjijñānaśakuntalam*. Edited by M. R. Kale. Delhi: Motilal Banarsidass.

Kaushal, Molly, Alok Bhalla and Ramakar Pant, eds. 2015. *Ramkatha in Narrative, Performance and Pictorial Tradition*s. Delhi: Aryan Publications.

Kauṭilya. 1962. *The Arthaśāstra of Kauṭilya and the Cāṇakya sūtra*. Edited by Sri Vachaspati Gairola. Varanasi: Chowkhamba Vidya Bhavan.

Kipling, John Lockwood. 1904. *Beast and Man in India*. London: Macmillan & Co.

Korom, Frank J. 2006. *Village of Painters: Narrative Scrolls from West Bengal*. Santa Fe: Museum of New Mexico Press.

Krishnamachariar, M. 1974 [1937]. *History of Classical Sanskrit Literature*. 3rd ed. Delhi: Motilal Banarsidass.

Krishnan, Gauri Parimoo. 2010. *Ramayana in Focus: Visual and Performing Arts of Asia*. Singapore: Asian Civilizations Museum.

Krttivāsa. 1957. *Rāmāyaṇa Kṛttivāsa Viracita*. Edited by Harekrishna Mukhopadhyaya. Kalikata: Sahitya Samsad.

Losty, J.P. 2008. *Love and Valour in India's Great Epic: The Rāmāyaṇa*. London: The British Library.

McCutchion, David J. and Suhrid K. Bhowmik. 1999. *Patuas and Patua Art in Bengal*. Midnapore: Marang Buru Press; Calcutta: Firma KLM.

Olivelle, Patrick. 2013. *King, Governance, and Law in Ancient India: Kautilya's Arthasastra*. New York: Oxford University Press.

Rāya, Dāśarathī. 1997. *Dāśarathī Rāyera Pāñcālī*. Edited by Ardhendushekhar Ray. Kolkata: Mahesh.

Rāya, Jagadrāma, and Rāmaprasada Raya. 1996. *Rāmprasādī Jagadrāmī Rāmāyaṇa*. EdIted by Nirmalendu Mukhopadhyaya. Kolkata: Mahesh.

Rossi, Barbara. 1998. *From the Ocean of Painting: India's Popular Paintings, 1589 to the Present*. New York: Oxford University Press.

Santra, Tarapada. 2011. *Folk Arts of West Bengal and the Artist Community*, trans. Shankar Sen. New Delhi: Niyogi Books.

Sen, Dineshchandra. 1920. *The Bengali Ramayanas*. Calcutta: University of Calcutta.

Sen, Rajendra Nath, trans. 1920. *Brahmavaivarta Purāṇam*. Allahabad: The Panini Office, Bhuvaneshwari Ashram. Reprinted, New York: AMS Press, 1974

Singh, Kavita. 2011. "What's New in Pata Painting?" In Dallapiccola 2011: 6279.

Smith, W. L. 1988. *Rāmāyaṇa Traditions in Eastern India: Assam, Bengal and Orissa*. Stockholm: Department of Indology, University of Stockholm.

Varadpande, M.L. 1992. *History of Indian Theatre*. Vol. 2. Delhi: Abhinav Publications.

Vijayan, K. 1997. *Rāmāyaṇa in Palm Leaf Pictures: Citrarāmāyaṇa*. Thiruvantapuram: Oriental research Institute and Manuscripts Library, University of Kerala. [Reprinted 2000].

Viśākhadatta. 1969. *Mudrārākṣasa*. Edited by R.S. Tripathi. Varanasi: Viswavidyalaya Prakashan.

index

S